One Move Ahead

THE REMARKABLE LIFE OF T.B.F. THOMPSON

with

DERICK BINGHAM

AMBASSADOR

One Move Ahead
First published 1995 by Ambassador Productions Ltd.
Copyright © 1995 T.B.F. Thompson
Reprinted December 1995

*Proceeds from the sale of this book will be used to further
Christ's kingdom at home and abroad*

AMBASSADOR PRODUCTIONS

Providence House
16 Hillview Avenue,
Belfast, BT5 6JR
Northern Ireland

Emerald House Group, Inc.
1 Chick Springs Road, Suite 102
Greenville, South Carolina, 29609

Contents

About The Author

DERICK BINGHAM is a graduate of Queen's University, Belfast and is a columnist with the "Belfast Telegraph" and "The Christian Herald". He recently received a major award in the United States for "Writing which presents in a sensitive thought provoking manner the biblical position on issues affecting the world today." This biography is his 13th book. He is also a full-time Bible Teacher with the Crescent Church in the University district of South Belfast where he teaches a weekly Bible Class, now approaching its 19th year, which is attended by people from all walks of life. He also teaches similar monthly Bible Classes in Glasgow and Edinburgh and has an extensive speaking schedule across the UK and overseas for the purpose of teaching of the Scriptures.

Foreword

By THE LORD CHANCELLOR
The Right Honourable The Lord Mackay of Clashfern

**House of Lords,
London SW1A OPA**

THIS IS A FASCINATING ACCOUNT OF THE BUSINESS
life of T.B.F. Thompson but for me its principal interest lies in
the account of the part his Christianity had in it.

He clearly, after his conversion, based his business activities
on his Christian world view. He was indeed one whom his
religion made trustworthy. I have seldom seen a stronger
recommendation than that given him by his bank after a long
course of dealing with him and with intimate knowledge of his
transactions.

I also think that the fact he assembled dealerships for so many
competing companies in one site, and particularly in his own

business, showed not only innovation but also a high degree of trust from the manufacturers for whom he dealt - and also from the large number of customers he supplied.

He knew deep sorrow as well as business success and in that sorrow he sought the good of others by recounting the Christianity of his late first wife, Kathleen on a tape recording made after her passing.

There is no better testimony to the truth of the Christian faith than a life which manifests the influence of that faith. T.B.F. Thompson was one move ahead so often in business. He has given us a fine example to follow also in the field of Christian practice.

Mackay of Clashfern

Preface

HE DETESTED SCHOOL AND COULDN'T GET OUT OF it quickly enough; he was later awarded the highest degree the leading university in his native Province had to offer. He started out collecting eggs and selling groceries to farmers up and down the countryside around Garvagh in County Londonderry; he became, later, the joint owner of what is reputed to be the largest farm in Ireland, the 3,160 acre Grianan Estate in County Donegal. The Estate contained the ancient stone fort known as Grianan of Aileach, thought to date from 1700 B.C. It was the Royal Court of Kings and was, in fact, the scene of one of St. Patrick's most notable victories over Paganism. He bought the farm, with his partners, in Geneva, Switzerland without ever having first seen it!

He persuaded his father, a general merchant, to give up the horse and cart and switch to a lorry. He innovated by putting a tank with a tap under the seat of the lorry and instead of the folk having to come into town for paraffin, he took the paraffin to them; later he was to own fuel oil distribution companies.

From taxi-ing honeymooners from the Imperial Hotel, in Garvagh in County Londonderry to sea-side resorts in his father's Model T Ford, to owning the Rolls-Royce car franchise for Northern Ireland; from hauling sand and gravel to build runways for aerodromes during World War 2, to owning a major construction company like Farrans; the life of Thomas Bacon French Thompson is not a boring one. He deposited £25.00 in his first bank account with the Northern Bank which didn't even have a branch in his native Garvagh, but was represented by an agency on two days of the week. Later he was to direct diverse commercial outlets with a combined turnover of around £200 million per annum. Not bad for a fellow who left school at 15.

In an astute novel of Alabama life by Fannie Flagg, there is a very memorable character called Idgie Threadgoode. Idgie had a sharp business mind but her most famous ability was for putting her hands into a bee's nest swarming with thousands of worker bees and pulling out honey without being stung, and, all as calm as you like. Idgie would then give the honey to others. She was affectionately known as "The Bee Charmer".

When I was asked to write this biography, I expected to find a man at the top of a huge commerical enterprise who would be a very complex individual, at best, paranoid, at worst, a nervous wreck!

The closer I got to him the more I found him to be at peace with himself, at peace with God and full of a sense of fun and laughter. He was surrounded by a hornet's nest of a Province filled with the bombing and killing and wrecking of terrorists determined to bring the commerical life of Northern Ireland to a standstill. I found Dr. Thompson to have the ability to put his hands right into the whole hornet's nest and get honey out. Not just honey for himself but honey to share with the people who were in great need. The more I investigated his life, the more I discovered stories of people he had helped who were far removed from the world of multi-million pound deals.

Northern Ireland is very famous for being the birthplace of the defibrillator, invented by the indefatigable Professor Pantridge. I discovered the "Bee Charmer" had been busy at work supplying defibrillators to doctors in hospitals at his own expense. I discovered him directing a small medical company in support of the innovative work done at Queen's University and Musgrave Park Hospital. I found him having a keen interest in and support of the Waveney Hospital Cardiac Unit, in Ballymena, County Antrim and discovered that he is a board member of the Ulster Independent Clinic in Belfast.

I found him employing a husband-and-wife team who spend all their time visiting the elderly and the sick at home, in hospital, or in community care. I saw a holiday home built to four star hotel standard in Portstewart in County Londonderry where each year approximately five hundred people in need enjoy the benefit of a week's free holiday by the sea, regardless of religious or political affiliation. On and on it goes, the story of a philanthropist driven by his often quoted maxim; "I don't want to be the richest man in the cemetery!"

I have seen this "Bee Charmer" at work when a phonecall came in giving a report of terrorist activity in one of his companies. "Was anybody hurt?", he asked, "Were any jobs lost?". Quick, right to the point, no nonsense. His powers of concentration on any project in hand are truly amazing. Avoiding minor obstacles he tackles the big ones and more often than not he removes them to extract the honey.

I suppose tycoons and their circle are often looked on as F. Scott Fitzgerald portrayed some of their lifestyles in 'The Great

Gatsby'; "Drifting here and there, unrestfully, wherever people played polo and were rich together ...... careless people...... (who) smashed up things and creatures and then retreated back into their money or their vast carelessness or whatever it was that kept them together, and let other people clean up the mess they had made". This tycoon is not from such a mould. John D. Rockefeller once said,"The poorest man I know is the man who has nothing but money". I hope to prove that Dr. Thompson has a lot more than money

It was the Lake District poet, William Wordsworth who believed that "The child is the father of the man". Any biographer worth his or her salt will look very carefully at the childhood of their subject to find traits which will, inevitably, become permanent characteristics. I found that the young Tom Thompson was an outstanding draughts player, eventually representing his town in competitions. The trait was certainly in his family and can be found there to this day. Young Tom's father had a draughts-board move which became rather famous in Garvagh and district. It was known as "The Thompson Square". It was a square on the draughts- board where he always tried to place one of his men. When he landed on it he arranged other pieces around the board to defend the square from assault. Where was it? It lay on the left hand side of the board and by moving a "left hand" draughts piece diagonally two moves to the right, the almost unassailable square could be reached. Future generations of players were warned to keep "Grandpa Thompson" off his square at all costs!

Young Tom was not slow at learning draughts-board moves from his father and developed a few of his own which made him quite formidable. Imagine the scene many years later as "T.B.F." on a number of occasions challenged young and enthusiastic business executives to a game of draughts and promised them and their families "a trip to the Continent, all expenses paid, the best of good food and no strong drink", if they beat him. They sat down at the draughts board with "relish" written all over their faces dreaming no doubt of Venice and Paris and Stockholm. But sadly, all was only a dream and they would have to waken up to reality for "T.B.F." was, characteristically, always one move ahead!

He has taken a lot of "kings" in a row, betimes, and the players who owned the "kings" were not always glad to see them go. They were, though, fairly won by a very astute player called, recently, by a University Professor, "one of the top four players in business in Northern Ireland in the last fifty years".

Has he any faults? Yes, but Scroogitis is not one of them. When questioning one of Northern Ireland's leading accountants about his longstanding business relationship with Dr. Thompson, I asked him to sum up what he thought marked him most. Without a flinch he replied, "Generosity of spirit". I would ask you to note that this is no "goody two shoes" story. To present it as such would make it unreal and untrue. Rumours have long persisted that he made his money in smuggling. Though it is true that at one stage of his life he smuggled, I want to show that his money did not come from smuggling and that at his conversion to Christ in 1947 such malpractice was decidedly left behind for the rest of his life. Questions have to be asked as to whether or not he made major mistakes. The answer is that he certainly did, particularly in the 1950's. Mistakes were made that brought him to the edge of disaster in business. But he survived. Survived to leave the little town of Garvagh where he was born above a shop on its Main Street to make his way to Buckingham Palace to be appointed an Officer of the Order of the British Empire by Her Majesty, Queen Elizabeth II.

He survived to become the High Sheriff of the County of Londonderry following a long succession of outstanding leaders who go right back to the appointment of Robert Columb in

1600. Survived to extract more honey to share with "the hidden ones"; the suffering, the harassed, the victims, the lonely, the hurting.

But then, we are rushing ahead too much; we need to go back, back to where it all started and to learn how Dr. T.B.F. Thompson became the epitome in his generation of King Solomon's famous proverb. The proverb? "See a man diligent in his business? He shall stand before kings".

Derick Bingham
Belfast, 1995

◆ CHAPTER ONE ◆

"A rough place"

THERE IS, IN LIFE, NO SUCH THING AS AN ORDINARY person. Equally there is no such thing as an ordinary place. Investigate any community from Paris to Pucket's Creek, from Geelong to Garvagh and you will find out things you wouldn't even dream of. Take Garvagh, for instance, situated in the County of Londonderry, some ten miles south of the inland port of Coleraine and thirty-one miles east of the city of London-derry. Garvagh consists, for the most part, of a long and very wide main street. You could drive through it in less than five minutes. But towns are about people, and people have been around Garvagh for a very long time. The famous "Kerwin Beads" found at Kerwin Moss, near Garvagh, were worn by people who held an important position in the district 1,500 years before the birth of Christ.

It was probably because she did not hold an important position, or, at least, a wealthy one that got a very pretty young woman into trouble when she fell in love with the son of Garvagh's most famous citizen of the time. Her lover's father, Stratford Canning, lived at the Castle just south of the town. The

Castle was a spacious mansion with six hundred acres of land attached. The local High School now stands where the Castle once stood and its grounds are now Garvagh Forest Park.

The pretty girl was an actress called Mary Ann Costello from County Mayo and because she was penniless, Stratford Canning banished his son for being associated with her. They married and settled in London in abject poverty where they ran a boarding-house for actors. Their son, George, through the kindness and care of his uncle, eventually went to Eton and developed a flair for public speaking. He went up to Christ Church, Oxford, where he became an oustanding scholar and a formidable debater. He became a great friend of the British Prime Minister, William Pitt, and under his guidance entered Parliament in 1793. He became British Foreign Secretary in 1807 and by his brilliance greatly frustrated the plans of Napoleon. George, unfortunately, had his political career interrupted following a dispute with the War Minister, Viscount Castlereagh. This led to a duel fought between the two men in September 1809 in which George was injured in the thigh. He then resigned from the Government and had to endure seven years in the political wilderness before regaining his seat at the Cabinet table. On the 6th August, 1822, Castlereagh committed suicide and George succeeded his political rival as Foreign Secretary and Leader of the House of Commons. He always maintained a deep interest in Irish affairs and he was a life-long campaigner for Catholic emancipation.

In April 1827, following the retirement of Lord Liverpool, George Canning became First Lord of the Treasury, Prime Minister and Chancellor of the Exchequer. Sadly, George died suddenly on the 8th August, 1827 after only four months in office. He was buried the following week in Westminster Abbey next to the grave of his friend and mentor, William Pitt. There is no question that he remains one of the most impressive, brilliant and illustrious politicians of the early 19th century.

Fathers really ought to be very careful when they refuse to let their sons come home; even, in Garvagh. The last three centuries of history in Garvagh is tied very closely with the Canning family. Unlike most of the towns and villages of County Londonderry, Garvagh was not built by one of the London companies but was a private development of the Canning family. Garvagh is the centre of an area of great prehistoric interest having an iron age fort just north of the town known as "The Moat", reckoned to have been used as a signal station to warn local chiefs of impending danger. There are many burial sites around the town and clay pots have been found from time to time containing the ashes and bones of ancient inhabitants going back for at least four thousand five hundred years

Like most towns and villages in Ireland, Garvagh is named in Irish meaning, "a rough place". It was just that when the first British settlers arrived in the area finding no roads, no bridges, no fields, and only round huts of a design not changed in over a thousand years.

After the Great Rebellion of 1641, George Canning, an agent of the Ironmonger's Company in London acquired the townland of Garvagh, privately from a local chief called Gilduffe McBrian O'Cahan. The townland was a native freehold and as such could not be developed by "The Planters", as they became known. Local tradition has it that it cost George Canning nothing to acquire the land since it was won as the result of a reckless gamble. O'Cahan, in a drunken dispute, is said to have signed away his entire property in the conviction that he was right. Canning then very shrewdly lodged the paper with his solicitor and having proved that he had won the argument, he claimed the property. There may be some truth in this story, for although the Ironmongers state that Canning had bought the townland of Garvagh from O'Cahan, they could not produce any deed to confirm it.

It would appear more likely that George Canning gained the land when it became a forfeit because of O'Cahan's part in the Rebellion. One thing is very clear; it was George Canning's son, Paul, who started the new town of Garvagh on its present site.

Amongst other things he built a Parish Church in 1659. This Parish Church has had a long list of outstanding Rectors, probably the most famous being Rev. George Alexander who was the father of Dr. William Alexander, Bishop of Derry and Raphoe, whose wife wrote the famous Christian hymn, "There is a green hill far away, without a city wall". The hymn was, of course, suggested to her by the walls of Londonderry. In the hearth tax roll of 1662, there are seventeen householders named who have a hearth and are paying tax in Garvagh. John Chambers, Robert Solesby, John Cunningham, William Cann, Charles McCotter, Andrew Alexander, Robert Mulligan, Hugh Smith, Hugh O'Doherty, Alexander Christie, Robert Gault, John Philips, Donnighie McPhillips, James Clydesdale, Edward Townsend, John Woodrow and Janet Halsby. These seventeen householders and their families made a very good start to the town.

In life there is certainly no need to go looking for trouble for trouble comes looking for us, and the good citizens of Garvagh were soon to learn through a dispatch rider ,who brought a letter to George Canning at the Castle, that a Rebellion was imminent. It caused panic amongst Garvagh's first citizens and the settlers quickly departed to seek shelter behind the walls of Londonderry. Eventually life returned to the village.

Throughout the ebbs and flows of history, people continued to settle in Garvagh and by 1725 we find that Garvagh has developed into a town of fifty-five houses, with a market and a mill. We find that Stratford Canning was then building four two-storied and six single-storied houses. He was also dividing the land near the tenant's houses by stone walls into twenty areas of one acre each and the rest of the townland into larger fields of four, five or six acres. When we arrive into the nineteenth century, we find Cannings still living at Garvagh and not only becoming famous because of George, who had become British Prime Minister, but also because of other members of the family who were making a name for themselves, the most notable being Earl Canning who was appointed First Viceroy of India in 1858. He was a man of great tact and moderation and his behaviour following the Indian Mutiny was to earn him the nickname "Clemency Canning". The English upper class disapproved of Canning's leadership and thought he was soft but in fact he was setting an example, which, if it had been followed, would have resulted in far better ties between Britain and India than currently exists.

No biography of any Garvagh citizen, no matter how famous, would be complete without some reference to the famous battle of Garvagh of July 26th, 1813. While the "battle" was a very minor event in the overall history of Ireland, a song written about it has placed Garvagh very clearly into the public imagination. Local legend has it that the song was composed by a local tramp and sold in adjoining fairs and at public gatherings, printed as a broadsheet.

It reads;

The night before the July fair,
The *Ribbonmen they did prepare
For three miles round to wreck and tear
And burn the town of Garvagh;
The torey whistle loud and shrill,
We heard it o'er the high Mourne Hill,
Fall on brave boys we'll slay and kill,
The Protestants of Garvagh.

The day came on they did repair,
In multitudes to Garvagh fair,
Some travelled thirty miles or mair,
To burn the town of Garvagh.
They all appeared in greatest haste,
White handkerchiefs tied round their waists,
But their jackets we did soundly baste,
That July fair in Garvagh.

To Coleraine strait away we went,
For aid but none to us they sent,
This bloody crew all to prevent
From their designs in Garvagh.
To 'Pruviance then we quick applied,
For aid which he soon us denied,
Saying: "Longest stands the toughest hide"
I'll find no aid for Garvagh.

The Protestants and the Orangemen
Like brothers did assemble then,
To keep the town was their design,
Or die like men in Garvagh;
We fired blank shots of no avail,
Then orange balls they flew like hail,
While Ribbonmen soon turned their tail,
With deadly wounds from Garvagh.

Then Captain Douay cried: "Brave boyes",
Maintain your cause and fear no noise,
We'll massacre these Orange boys
And burn the town of Garvagh.
Sure he had not turned himself well round,
Till he received a deadly wound,
His heels went up and his head went down
At the third tree in Garvagh.

We gave the word to clear the street,
While numbers flew like hunted sheep,
Then Protestant did Papist meet
At Davidson's in Garvagh.
Oh the brave boys if you had seen,
'Twas their best men through Ballinameen,
While Orange boys pursued them keen,
And cleared the town of Garvagh.

But mark what followed this affray,
They thought to swear our lives away,
To jail we went without delay,
We had no guards from Garvagh;
They horrid oaths against us swore,
Such swearing you never heard before,
Why McCluskey swore three hours or more,
Against the boys of Garvagh.

The Judge he would have us condemned
Had it not been for our jurymen
Our grateful thanks is due to them
For they cleared the boys of Garvagh.
All thanks and praise we will render still,
To Mr. Price and to brave George Hill
And the Beresford who is with us still
For they cleared the boys of Garvagh.

Many have been the events and many have been the colour-
ful characters passing through Garvagh and none more famous
than Dennis Hempson born at Craigmore, near Garvagh in the
year 1695 who, despite being blinded by smallpox at the age of
three, was to become one of the greatest harpists that Ireland
has produced in modern times. Hempson died at the age of 112
and he had played the harp to earn his living for one hundred
years of his life!

No town or community is without its history and the history
is made by its people. Whether it be the stories of battles and
feuds of long ago, of hard times and good times, people are very
much at the centre of all of the sea-changes that different
generations bring with them. Few of Garvagh's inhabitants,
though, had any notion of the commercial sea-changes that
were to be instigated by the little boy born to Tom and Sadie
Thompson on Main Street on May 20th, 1915. His is our story.

Note:
* Ribbonmen was the name given to a secret Nationalist society.
* Alex Pruviance was the RM in Garvagh at the time of the battle and as such had power
  to call out the military to keep the peace.

Prime Minister George Canning at the height of his powers. His Garvagh connections make a fascinating story.
(Picture reproduced by the kind permission of Garvagh High School)

"T.B.F." aged 1 year and 3 months, with his brother Billy.

*"T.B.F's" parents, Tom and Sadie Thompson in a family portrait with
Billy and Tom, junior!*

"T.B.F." with, for once, time on his hands! His brother Billy wears the famous Edwardian "sailor's suit" of the period.

Our subject begins to grow.

♦ CHAPTER TWO ♦

"Wee Johnnie Funny"

HIS PARENTS CALLED HIM THOMAS BACON FRENCH Thompson. French? It seems his mother was deeply affected by the hellish war raging in France at the time of his birth. Young men from the County and island in which she lived were going out to fight the German Army in France and Flanders. They were to be exposed to poison gas, massed machine-gun fire and the strafing aeroplanes. They were to live with rats and lice and the stench of decaying flesh, to stare up at the sky by day and to venture out only by night.

The British Army on The Western Front in 1915 lived in candle-lit dugouts and trenches hewn from Fricourt chalk or La Basse clay. Their officers studied new gadgets called wrist-watches before blowing their zero-hour whistles and the soldiers hurled themselves "over the top" towards aprons of wire with barbs as thick as a man's thumb and to face a murderous hail of bullets; in one attack the price of 700 yards was 26,000 men.

Mrs. Thompson didn't want to forget the sacrifice of incredibly brave men who were dying in France and so she added the name "French" to her little boy's name.

While, on an average day on the Western Front, 2,533 men on both sides were killed in action, 9,121 were wounded and 1,164 went missing, little Tom Thompson faced his first years of human life on Main Street, Garvagh. His father, who had been brought up on a small farm at Tamneymore, outside the town, served his apprenticeship to the grocery and hardware trade in Robinson's Shop, Garvagh. He worked for the first five years for no payment. In his sixth year he was paid £20.00 and afterwards received small rises until the twentieth year when he received the grand sum of £50.00. He often told people that he had never earned £1.00 in a week in his whole working life! It was all too true. In all of his married life he never slept a single night out of his own home.

Tom's father was an extremely fit individual and very popular with the public. He would think nothing of jumping on his bicycle and cycling to the town of Cookstown and entering for a bicycle race. He was not unknown either for jumping over the counter of the shop in which he was employed. Young Tom, though, could never be accused of having been born with a silver spoon in his mouth.

The only connection he had in childhood with the famous founders of Garvagh, the Canning family, was a rocking horse which he just loved to play on over at Garvagh's Imperial Hotel. Paul Canning's son, George, has been given the title "Lord Garvagh" in 1818, and the title has now passed down through succeeding generations of the family right up to the fifth and present Baron Garvagh. Young Tom's pride and joy was Lord Garvagh's rocking horse which was "stabled" in a store at the back of the Imperial Hotel. The young boy became firm friends with the owner's son, Billy Fitzsimmons, and many were their adventures together. The Imperial Hotel was THE place to stay in Garvagh and its residents were regularly transferred to Garvagh Station by the intrepid Willie Johnston who drove the hotel's jaunting car.

Tom's was an uncomplicated childhood, far removed from the fast moving technological age he was to invade. Traffic was virtually nil on Main Street, Garvagh and his childhood days were filled with playing Hop Scotch and ball games in the Ball Alley. There were, of course, the inevitable games of marbles played to the "Marley Code" in deadly earnest.

"There were "chalkies" and there were "stonies",
And many home made phoneys.
Some were made of putty, some of clay,
Some were a disaster,
They were made of alabaster,
When you hit them they would break away."

Garvagh is built on the west side of the river Agivey and many an hour young Tom and his friends would spend crossing and re-crossing the famous stepping stones on the river. At the time of the first settlement and for many a year afterwards, the only way to cross the Agivey was by using the ancient fords and their adjoining stepping stones. Tom's stepping stones were above the existing bridge at the East side of Bridge Street, said to be the site of an ancient ford.

As a child he loved to play court tennis and table tennis, to walk on stilts and throw horseshoes. Recently the game of horseshoe throwing has had a very public profile as the recent American President George Bush and his staff played it quite regularly in a corner of the White House Garden. Tom's horseshoe throwing competitions were not held in such auspicious surroundings. When snow fell on Garvagh young Tom could be found sleighing full tilt down Dan's Brae and along the street to McNeary's Corner. He well remembers his cousin, Alfie Mann, who lived next door in Main Street, asking his brother Billy to "go up to Carrie's for a ha'penny 'ock". It certainly proves a stick of rock in Tom's childhood knew nothing about inflation.

Every year he would go off on holiday with his mother for a week to stay in Enfield Terrace, Portstewart. He loved to fish in the harbour for "spricklybags" and was almost killed one day when he fell down the stairs in the holiday guest house. On such everyday events does the thin line of life or death run. Perhaps, though, the treats he most enjoyed were visits to his mother's home at Gorticastle in County Tyrone.

Things slowly began to improve for the family, materially. In 1924 when Tom was nine, his father bought the corner property known as the McNeary Corner, Garvagh. It had two houses attached with a shop, a yard, and gardens. Its price at auction was put down at £2,250 to Tom's father which, in those days, was no mean sum. There had been at least one other keen bidder for the property and afterwards he apologised for "putting the price up" and offered to assist in the payment. Tom's father would have none of it and proudly stated that he could make the payment. The property was renovated and the family moved in to their new home and business premises in 1925.

The family was an extended one. With father Tom and mother Sadie, young Tom and his brother Billy, there lived Mr. T. B. Thompson's brother, William and Mrs. Thompson's sister, Dolly. Gentle, helpful, and dedicated "Auntie Dolly", as she was known, helped in the home as well as in the shop.

She brought a sweetness with her personality everywhere she went and she did not waste her sweetness for it touched young Tom very deeply and, next to his mother, few women were to be thought of as highly throughout his lifetime. She was very close to Tom and often affectionately described him as the lad who was "always away to play golf with his golf bag trailing on the ground".

Garvagh no longer boasts of a golf course but in young Tom's day there was a nine hole course in the town and Tom caddied for players, earning many a half crown. He also collected golf balls which had been lost by players. The course may not have been designed by Jack Nicklaus or have a club house like Turnberry but it did have a railway carriage which served as the club house and a little lad who regularly came trudging up the hill trailing his golf bag behind him.

Tom, of course, played more than golf. Of an evening he and his friends loved to tie strong thread to the door-knockers of houses and then take the thread across to the other side of the street. A good tug on the thread brought householders to their doors to find no-one awaiting them. Poor Mary Lamont was often the victim of the invisible door-knockers and the boys just loved to get Mary mad. The same boys from Garvagh would quite often place a small tin or jug of water against the door, knock it and run for it. When the door opened the tin or jar of water fell over inside the door spilling all over the floor. It was mischievious but it was a far cry from modern times when old people are regularly beaten up by youngsters across the nation and robbed. Water and door-knocking were quickly forgiven in the 1920's.

Tom's brother, Billy, kept pet rabbits and was a first-rate shot with an air-gun. This fact was not always appreciated by his friends. His cousin, Alfie Mann, was bending over one day and suddenly got a nasty shock when a pellet from Billy's air-gun hit him in the backside. "Billy Thompson, Billy Thompson", he cried as he chased Billy down Garvagh Street, "I'll kill you! I'll kill you!" Billy survived to become a great sportsman and an outstanding and patient fisherman and to have the distinction of never leaving Ireland in his life. He was Tom's great protector in his childhood days for Tom, hating school, became, as time went on, a frequent "mitcher". This inevitably drew him into constant trouble with his teacher. Young Tom was not averse to playing snooker for money, either; a practice his parents vigorously opposed. Billy, time and again, protected his "wee brother" from many a punishment he richly deserved!

If, as C. S. Lewis said of the white witches' kingdom, that it was "always winter and never Christmas", then Tom and Billy Thompson did not live in such a kingdom. Christmas was the fun time of the year for the lads and like millions of other children they gleefully sent notes up the chimney for Santa Claus to let him know what was wanted most. It was the night of nights in their year. In pre-television days, of course, the Christmas Rhymers were at their prime and the showman in young Tom was not idle. Off he would go out into the country, walking for miles with his friends and putting on little plays in the country homes along the way. Kenneth Branagh or Lord Olivier never got to playing these theatrical productions but the Garvagh Christmas Rhymers were experts at these little shows. Of all the homes Tom visited in a night, and that was quite a few, Tom's favourite was the home of the McCausland Family. Why? They paid well! The lads would troop up the long drive, Tom with his little doctor's bag in his hand and all of them dressed up so that no-one would recognise who was participating. They would be ushered into the large drawing room with its blazing fire and friendly occupants and suddenly one of the lads would fall to the ground pretending to be ill. A dialogue followed the following invariable pattern;

Tom: "Here comes I - wee Doctor Brown",
              The best wee doctor in the town.

Patient: "What's your cure doctor?"

Tom: "The juice of the beetle,
      The sap of the tongs,
      The hard blade of the smoothing iron,
      Put that together with a white hen's bleather,
      Stirred up with a green duck's feather,
      And in three days you'll be all right."

Another stalwart production concerned Beelzebub and the intrepid Wee Johnnie Funny. Tom relished playing the part of Wee Johnnie Funny. Tom's friend Joe Gilmore would say;

"Here comes I - Beelzebub,
 Over my shoulder I carry my club,
 In my hand a frying pan,
 If you don't believe what I say,
 I'll leave Wee Johnny Funny to clear the way."

Inevitably Tom would follow with;

"Here come I - Wee Johnnie Funny,
 I'm the man that takes the money.
 All silver - no brass,
 Bad ha'pence won't pass."

If ever there were lines which were prophetic in a child's life, the lines of Wee Johnnie Funny prophesied Tom's future for he would one day be, indeed, the man who took the money. Whether it was charging a penny to see his cinematograph show on his mother's kitchen table or lifting a half crown with the Christmas Rhymers, the child was indeed the father of the man.

He may have looked very cute when a young boy in the suit made for him by dressmaker Mrs Johnston and the future Mrs. Troy of the famous County Londonderry newspaper family, but it is worth pointing out that he was more than cute, he proved to be very shrewd. He was, even in childhood, an outstanding draughts player and adept at always keeping a move ahead of the other fellow. Underlying this shrewdness his friend Billy Fitzsimmons always said that as a child Tom had a very great sense of the value of something. "He would," says Billy on hindsight, "have sold his school cap!" He was to sell a lot more than that in Garvagh within a very short span of years.

"T.B.F." at Garvagh Primary School, second left, front row.
The Master was not in good form!

Billy and Ruby's wedding with "T.B.F." as Best Man and Olive Moore as Bridesmaid.

◆ CHAPTER THREE ◆

"The entrepreneur"

"COME WITH ME, CHARLIE", SAID THE LONG RANGY man, "I want to show you something".

Henry Ford led his model making Danish woodworker employee, Charles Sorenson to the top floor of the Ford Motor Company headquarters in Dearborn, Michigan. Henry never really liked blueprints but always found it much easier to work with models. "I'd like to have a room finished off right here in this space", he said, "Put up a wall with a door in it big enough to run a car in and out. Get a good lock for the door .... we're going to start a completely new job."

The new job was the creation of a car which was to revolutionize the lives of millions of people. When the car finally went on the market at the beginning of October 1908, the wildest predictions for it were fulfilled. By the end of the winter Ford had to announce that the Company could not take any more immediate orders for their new Model T Ford, for the moment.

In 1909-10 Ford sold 18,664 Model Ts; in 1910-11 they sold 34,528; in 1911-12, an incredible 78,444 cars were sold and still the orders came in. Through the early 1920s the Model T sold consistently above the 1 million mark and by May 26, 1927, 15 million Model Ts rolled off the Dearborn assembly line.

"You know, Henry", wrote the farmer's wife to Henry Ford, from Georgia, "Your car lifted us out of the mud. It brought joy into our lives. We loved every rattle in its bones".

They loved it down at Thompson's Corner, Garvagh, too. When T.B. Thompson bought his Model T Ford, registered IW 610, it was the first car in Garvagh. Young Tom just couldn't keep his hands off it. The local police sergeant turned a very blind eye to the twelve year old lad who sneaked his father's Model T around the sideroads of Garvagh. This beginning proved to be a life-long fascination with cars and speed. One day Tom would own his Rolls Royces and his Jaguars but his father's "Tin Lizzy", as the Model T was affectionately known, has held a place in his memory and imagination like no other car.

By the end of the First World War almost half the cars on earth were Model Ts. The car transformed the way people lived and as Henry Ford himself stated, it was large enough for the family and small enough for the individual to run and care for. Perhaps, though, the writer E.B. White has best summed up how this amazing car was started. You had to be careful not to put your thumb around the starting handle, for, if you did, you risked breaking an arm or wrist:

"The trick was to leave the ignition switched off, proceed to the animal's head, pull the choke (which was a little wire protruding through the radiator) and give the crank two or three nonchalant upward lifts. Then, whistling as though thinking about something else, you would saunter back to the driver's cabin, turn the ignition on, return to the crank, and this time, catching it on the down stroke, give it a quick spin with plenty of That. If this procedure was followed the engine almost always responded - first with a few scattered explosions, then with a tumultous gunfire, which you checked by racing around to the driver's seat and retarding the throttle. Often, if the emergency brake hadn't been pulled all the way back, the car advanced on you the instant the first explosion occurred, and you would hold it back by leaning your weight against it. I can still feel my old Ford nozzling me at the kerb, as though looking for an apple in my pocket".

As the petrol engine invaded and changed Western civilization, so too did an invention of Henry Ford's friend, Thomas Eddison. Young Tom Thompson's mother loved her son very much but she was once heard to say that she reckoned Tom could never earn his own living. She was as wrong about her boy as Eddison's schoolteacher proved to be. As a boy Eddison had a great deal of imagination and curiosity, and was taken away from school because the teacher thought his continual questions were a sign of stupidity. None of us regret young Eddison's questions today for they led to the invention of the electric light bulb.

At Garvagh in the early 1930's, Sam Stewart's generator supplied all the electricity needs of the people of the town. The electric light bulb in young Tom Thompson's room, however, never burnt late for his studies. He simply detested school. In fact he spent many hours playing billiards at the Imperial Hotel and snooker at Marcus Dickson's. Master Moore and his assistant, Miss Jeannie Wallace, did their best but Tom was no "swot"! When he moved on to the Model School in Coleraine and eventually the Coleraine Academical Institution, it was the buses and the business that lay behind them that seemed to interest young Tom far more than the studies they took him to every day. He can still reel off the names of the rival companies and the models of buses they owned.

It was a Mr. Gault who first started the bus service between Garvagh and Coleraine. His bus was called a "Vulcan" and had solid tyres and when it went down Garvagh Street, the very bells in the bus rang as it went over the bumps! Mr. Gault's rivals were the Stewart Brothers, Harry and Joe. Their first bus was called a "Pheasant" and was quickly followed by two "Rio-Sprinters". Often when the buses were hired, Tom would go with Harry and Joe, not as a conductor, but, just for the ride and for what is euphemistically called in Northern Ireland, "the crack" (not to be confused with a modern drug of the same name!). Tom would sit "up front" with the driver Jack Mullan, brother of the late Garvagh businessman J. T. Mullan. The business of buses certainly caught his imagination much more than the plays of Shakespeare, the poems of Keats or any theorem by Pythagoras.

French verbs were never to rival the day when, under pressure from "the boys" the back door of the bus burst open on the way to school and young Willie McFetridge was only saved from certain death by young Tom and his friends holding on to his legs and pulling him back in again!

At school Tom had a teacher whose nickname was "Skip-a-line" because of his penchant for asking boys to "skip a line, leave a line or draw a double line " in their exercise books when he was dictating. Tom skipped more than a line, academically, and despite the pleadings of his parents he left school at fifteen and entered the university of life.

In 1930 he started working for his father who was, of course, a General Merchant in Garvagh. His father sold everything from tea, sugar and flour to animal feeding stuff, grass-seed and coal. The faithful Johnnie Moore, handyman of handymen, drove the T.B. Thompson & Son horse and cart to the railway station and brought back a lot of the goods and young Tom, donning a shop coat, served behind the counter.

They were very busy days with no real set hours. Tom's job was to serve the customers and to prepare the groceries for Bob Kirkwood's "grocery run". Bob had a horse and cart and took groceries around the countryside to the farmhouses and for about three years Tom organised this supply line. It was enjoyable work and the business was doing well, especially on a Saturday night when the farmer's wives would invade town for half pounds of tea and stones of flour and other essentials served at Thompson's Corner.

Life, though, turns on seemingly very small events and the decision of Bob Kirkwood to give up his "grocery run" did not seem a big change in Garvagh and district, but it was for young Tom. Bob gave very short notice to Mr. Thompson and he was suddenly faced with a major business decision. His son faced it for him and crossed his Rubicon. "We'll have no horse and cart, Dad", said Tom, "We'll buy a lorry and take over "the run" ourselves!"

Tom had become an entrepreneur and Northern Ireland was soon going to become networked with his acumen. It is worth asking as young Tom went up to Felix Doherty's home near Craigavole Roman Catholic Chapel to offer him £70.00 for his small Ford lorry, registration IW 3737; just what is an entrepreneur?

Professor Kenny in his interesting book *Out On Their Own: Conversations with Irish Entrepreneurs* quotes one definition of entrepreneurs as "being people who have the ability to see and evaluate business opportunities; to gather the necessary resources, to take advantage of them; and to initiate appropriate action to ensure success". As young Tom knocked Felix Doherty's door he was the epitome of Professor Kenny's definition. It proved to be the door to business fortune. Felix sold him the small Ford lorry for £70.00. Tom had two drawers fitted to its side and a drawer at the back, he came out from behind the counter and went off looking for business up and down the countryside. He was not long in finding it. T. B. F. Thompson, the entrepreneur, was on his way.

Tom could not, of course, have been on his way had it not been for the faithful dedication of his brother Billy who kept the family business running in Garvagh. Billy was always proud of his brother's business achievements but was, himself, happy to simply concentrate on running the Garvagh General Merchant Store. He was, in many ways very different to his brother Tom. He had a passionate interest in music and was a very accomplished pianist, organist and piano accordionist. In his early days he deputised at the church organ at his local Presbyterian Church and had a very keen ear, all his life, for music. Billy was a man of simple pleasures and just loved to hunt, shoot and fish. Many were the stories he could tell of adventures with his gun and fishing rod.

Billy, of course, was as open to Cupid's arrows as anyone else and he fell for Ruby Moore the daughter of a hill farmer. Ruby came from Co. Tyrone and was in the habit of visiting her sister who was a governess in Churchtown who lived about four miles outside Garvagh. Ruby held a post as a schoolteacher in Co. Tyrone.

Training for schoolteaching in Ruby's day was no cake-walk and money was very scarce. She used to recall how that when at Stranmillis Teacher Training College and wanting to see the animals at Bellevue Zoo at the other side of Belfast, she found she did not have the full bus fare to get her to the zoo. She simply paid the bus fare, one way, and walked it back to the Training College, a distance of approximately eight miles!

A teaching post was, of course, gold dust and Ruby was more than glad to get one. Ruby, though, soon faced another formidable problem. A rumour swept the Province that the Department of Education was going to introduce a rule that if female teachers got married, they were going to have to give up their jobs. Ruby's job was an absolute financial lifeline and she had by this time got engaged to Billy. The rumour was that teachers already married could retain their jobs. Ruby, understandably, panicked and immediately wired a telegram to Billy reading, "Wedding imperative" and named the date! The rumour that came from this telegram got poor Billy and Ruby into hot water, as can be easily imagined. As it turned out, the Department of Education did not introduce the rule.

Billy and Ruby were married at Mountjoy Presbyterian Church in Omagh and because of their financial situation it was decided that Ruby would keep her teaching post in Co. Tyrone while Billy ran the store in Co. Londonderry.

So it was that for the first six years of their marriage Billy "held the fort" at Garvagh while Ruby "taught the fort" in Co. Tyrone. Both their sons, Ivan and Kenneth, were born in Tyrone and their daughter, Valerie, was born in Garvagh.

Ivan distinctly recalls being called Ivan Moore on weekdays and Ivan Thompson on Sundays! Eventually Ruby got a post at Ballyagan Primary School near Garvagh and when it closed she was appointed Principal of Garvagh Primary School. The first class results she got from her pupils are legendary in the district to this day.

The family fondly recalls sleighing down Dan's Brae in Garvagh on snowy evenings piled on top of their father.

Garvagh even had a town sleigh which was a slow laborious contraption provided for families who did not have a sleigh of their own. Billy always enjoyed cruising past the contraption at break-neck speed and frequently enjoyed ditching his family in the ditch on the final corner of the run!

Billy was always marked with an outstandingly kind nature. Many were the families he literally helped with credit around Garvagh's hinterland. He knew he would get his money when the farmer's eggs or animals were sold, and, the books showed that his trust in the community was rewarded almost to the last penny.

It was gratifying to Billy that his older son, Ivan, joined him in the family business in 1959, which meant three generations of Thompsons had traded at the Corner in Garvagh. Some years after his father's death Ivan felt led to return to studies, which resulted in him leaving the grocery counter to take up a career in the classroom.

♦ CHAPTER FOUR ♦

"Smart boy wanted; last boy too smart"

To FIND BUSINESS IN 1934 WAS, OF COURSE, NO EASY matter. "T.B.F.", the entrepreneur, knew it, but, he had one quality which proved to be of great benefit; it was always a natural trait in him to have time for people. He was gregarious right from the start. Very seldom would you find him alone. He did not rake up and down the countryside on his grocery run taking what business he could without realising that the people he was dealing with had heartaches, worries and problems like people everywhere. He would spend a while chatting to them, listening to their problems and helping where he could. This quality was to stay with him right through his business life and when he reached the "big time", when people called him and he could not immediately see them he would always arrange to see them at a more convenient time. There was no "I'm-too-busy-to-see-you" syndrome. Up "The Glen" all of his customers were Roman Catholic folk and he also called every week at the Parochial House. "T.B.F." has never had any major problem in the area of community relations in a Northern Ireland pock-marked with them. Although many of his Protestant friends were in the Orange Order or the Freemasons, neither he, his brother nor his father ever belonged to either organisation. It did not hinder their progress in business in any way, at any time.

In the 1930s the big thing in the local General Merchant trade was, believe it or not, the price of what was known as "yellow meal". Any local General Merchant's reputation swung on the all famous and piercing question, "What's the price of your yellow meal?" It came in 2 cwt. bags. One day, up the street in Garvagh, drove the formidable Jimmy Blair with his cart full of feeding stuff, including the worthy Clarendo flour and of course the feeding stuff of feeding stuffs, "yellow meal". As Jimmy passed Tom's father on the street he shouted down the famous inevitable question. "Tom, what's the price of your yellow meal?" Mr. Thompson gave the correct price but Jimmy retorted that what he had obtained was far cheaper. Mr. Thompson pondered for a moment. "Can I see the rest of your bill, Jimmy?", he asked. When he read it he discerned that the yellow meal was certainly cheap but that the General Merchant who had sold Jimmy his cartload of provisions had bumped up the prices of other items to cover his loss on the "yellow meal". Mr. Thompson decided, on the spot, that the "yellow meal war" had better be sabotaged.

Most businessmen in the country explain their principles for living in the form of stories, especially in Ireland. The "yellow meal war" is described by "T.B.F." in the story of an advertisement for employment which appeared in a local paper, many years ago. It read, "Smart boy wanted; last boy too smart." "T.B.F.'s" father reckoned his local rival was being too smart, so, he decided to counter the "yellow meal" price imbalance. He told every customer on the "grocery run" that in future everyone would be paid the full price for their eggs without a single penny of profit going to "T.B. Thompson & Sons". To say that their business shot up is an understatement. The "yellow meal war" quickly receded! Soon, the lorry bought from Felix Doherty proved to be inadequate and a bigger lorry was purchased, a 30 cwt. Bedford, Registration IW 5645. Two drawers were fitted to the sides of the lorry and one at the rear. A large compartment for selling groceries and bread was also fitted. Underneath the driver's seat the ever innovative "T.B.F." put a large tank for selling paraffin oil with a little tap attached. "T.B.F." saw a market for taking paraffin oil to the farmer's wives rather than the farmer's wives having to come into town for it. His invariable companion, Johnny Linton, took care of the oil and feeding stuffs while he did the totting up and the weighing of eggs.

All eggs had to be weighed, in those days, as eggs were not sold by the dozen but were sold by weight. It was all a very busy time. Groceries were delivered on certain days, then the drawers were removed and feeding stuffs were delivered on other days, all on the same lorry. "T.B.F.", though, was not content with his country "grocery run" and decided to have a go at the creamery business. A bigger lorry was purchased, this time a 3 Ton Bedford Truck registered IW 5731 and "T.B.F." tendered at 1 1/8 pence per gallon to bring milk from the farms to the creamery. Willie Brown was the first driver employed to take on this work and although the creamery did not prove to be a big earner, it did help to get "T.B.F." into diversification. But again he was bored with it. His boredom threshold was always thin and he always kept his eye out for further business opportunities. He was not like the lad who emigrated to America and who, when he ran out of money, telegrammed his father. The telegram read, "No mon; no fun; your son". Back came an equally short telegram from his father, "Too bad; so sad; your Dad!". "T.B.F." didn't need to send any telegrams to his father. He simply contacted the local Potato Merchant in Garvagh, Mr. R. B. Lyttle asking him if it were possible to give him some haulage work.

Mr. Lyttle agreed and soon the 3 Ton Bedford headed for Belfast loaded with potatoes and brought back loads of feeding stuff from Belfast's great Milling Companies, E.T. Green's, John Thompson & Sons, White, Tompkins and Courage and Clow's. Loads of fertiliser were hauled as well and not a journey was wasted. "T.B.F." kept the books meticulously, much to Mr. Lyttle's delight, for "R.B." detested bookwork. A very good relationship built up between the ever expanding "T.B.F." and the much relieved R.B. Lyttle. The lorry, under the name "Thompson & Lyttle" on its side became a very familiar sight plying to and from Belfast. Not content with the R.B. Lyttle contract, "T.B.F." began hauling bags of lime from the mill situated just outside Garvagh. This required another lorry and this in turn helped "T.B.F." to extend his haulage involvement even further to bringing in supplies to Baxter's of Charlotte Street in Ballymoney. A typical day's run for "T.B.F's" driver, Bobby Brown, who was to be with him for 47 years, would involve a load of potatoes to Belfast, a return journey with feeding stuffs for Baxter's of Ballymoney, a delivery of bagged lime from the mill to various farmers around Garvagh and then back to Belfast for a further load.

His newly found and hard earned money brought him in 1936 the status symbol of all status symbols, a red MG two-seater sports car. He had driven his father's Model T around back roads in the countryside before he was even allowed a licence. He later drove commercial travellers to visit their contacts all over the country and also drove honeymooners from Garvagh to the seaside. He even drove the local hearse when required, but now, at 21, the red MG at Thompson's Corner was a reflection that he was going places.

A university student once asked the famous American Evangelist, Dr. Billy Graham, what he thought was the greatest surprise of his life. He immediately replied, "The brevity of life." Suddenly, just as life soared for the young "T.B.F." the reality of the brevity of life swept into his home; on 25th August, 1936, his beloved mother died. It broke his heart for he was exceptionally close to her and she had been his spiritual mentor. She had constantly witnessed to him of the peace she enjoyed through faith in Jesus Christ. She had often read the Scriptures to him and prayed with him and taught him that "The gift of God is Eternal Life through Jesus Christ our Lord".

He had often accompanied her to hear the Gospel preached and had never, at any time, thought its wonderful message irrelevant. Yet, he had neglected the spiritual side to his life and had not accepted Jesus Christ as his personal Saviour and Lord. With his mother gone, a very keen spiritual light went out in his home and Tom, though outwardly successful, was, in the words of Christ's parable, building his life on sand and not on the Rock of Ages. Business, of course, surged on and one year after his red MG had first roared around Garvagh, "T.B.F." set off with his friend, Harry Stewart, he of the Rio Sprinter buses, to London to purchase and collect a four-seater black MG, Registration CJJ 200 which he bought for £200.00. With a pounding heart he got behind the wheel of his new car and drove it from London to Liverpool and on to the steamer and home to Garvagh.

He began to gamble and take chances. One night in Portrush, he gambled all the money he had, £130.00. He even gave a loan to the establishment as he was gambling to help him gamble on! The next night he went back to try to win his own money back again but the police had shut the gambling down! He started to drift and a "Devil-may-care" attitude came into his life. He was troubled with varicose veins and a local G.P., Dr. Mooney, advised him to have an operation to have the offending veins removed. He went up to Belfast and had the operation performed by a surgeon called G. D. McFadden. He recuperated and returned to Garvagh and then had to return later to Belfast to have some injections and was distinctly warned to stay overnight in Belfast and rest. He had his injections but disobeyed doctor's orders and went and bought a bacon slicer for the shop and went home! He had gambled with his health and was soon to learn the cost; a very severe pain ensued and his temperature soared to 105 degrees. It dropped and soared again. A surgeon was called in and "T.B.F." found himself literally facing death. His father was so convinced his son was going to die that he shut the shop. The whole town waited for Tom's passing. There was no penicillin in those days and Nurse Fitzsimmons plied ice from the local butcher to try to stabilise "T.B.F.'s" temperature.

As he lay there facing the last great enemy, he promised God that if he lived he would live for Him. Like millions before him, when health returned, he forgot his vow. 1939 put "T.B.F." aside from business for six months. Just as he was recuperating from the most serious illness of his life, a British ultimatum to Hitler's Germany to withdraw its troops from Poland was ignored. At 11.15 a.m. on September 3rd, 1939 the British Prime Minister spoke to the nation over the B.B.C., telling them that Great Britain and Germany were once again at war. The lights certainly went out all over Europe. As Churchill put it in the House of Commons, "This is not a question of fighting for Danzig or fighting for Poland. We are fighting to save the whole world from the pestilence of Nazi tyranny and in defence of all that is most sacred to man. This is no war of domination or Imperial aggrandisement or material gain; no war to shut any country out of the sunlight and means of progress. It is a war, viewed in its inherent quality, to establish, on impregnable rocks, the rights of the individual, and it is a war to establish and revive the stature of man ...... We look forward to the day surely and confidently, when our liberties and rights will be restored to us, and when we will be able to share them with the peoples to whom such blessings are unknown". Millions of deaths were to occur before that day arrived.

"T.B.F." (on running board) ready to deliver!
From left: Johnny Linton, Roy McMillan and Willie Brown. The grocery
lorry's registration was AW 5645.

Thompson sells the Newforge Meal;
To all our customers we appeal
To buy a hundred weight and see
The effect of No. 1,2,3
No. 1 for the baby pig
No. 2 makes them grow so big,
No. 3 is for finishing off;
Try it and see how they lick the trough.

They fatten quicker and make less work;
The Newforge way for leaner pork;
You'll also be pleased when you see them weighed,
And for every pig you will get first grade.

Newforge Layer's mash makes hens lay
Larger eggs, and how they weigh!
Pigs or hens - they simply love it;
Buy Newforge and farm for profit.
Settle your troubles once and for all:
When in town give us a call;
It matters not where'er you deal
Only Thompson sells Newforge meal.

"T.B.F." and Pattison Nutt on the "Nile Steamer" on which they travelled 600 miles from Cairo to Luxor and on to Aswan.

"T.B.F." and Pattison Nutt astride donkeys at the Cataract Hotel, Aswan, December 1946.

♦ CHAPTER FIVE ♦

"Sugar and silk stockings"

HITLER HAD A FOUR-PHASE PLAN FOR THE invasion of Britain in 1940. In the first phase from July 10th to mid-August, the Luftwaffe were to win superiority in the air over the Channel and Southern England. The second phase lasted from mid-August to 7th September and the German aim was to destroy the R.A.F. fighting force by attacking its fighter planes and airfields. When Britain responded by bombing Germany, Hitler was so furious he ordered the Luftwaffe to bomb London, which they did 71 times between September 1940 and 16th May, 1941. In the final phase the Luftwaffe made night attacks on other major cities in the U.K., the first raid on Belfast coming on the night of 7th-8th April 1941. In comparison to other cities the raid was quite light and things soon returned to normal. On the night of 14th April, 1941, many of Belfast's citizens went to see a football match at Windsor Park between the Irish League and the League of Ireland or went to the cinema to see James Cagney at The Ritz in "Torrid Zone". The lull was a false one. The following day, Easter Tuesday, the siren sounded at 10.40 p.m. as the German planes approached. It was a clear night with no cloud and a light wind.

The planes approached from the North-West between the Blackmountain and Divis and went on bombing for seven hours. When they finally left at 5 a.m. they had killed almost 900 people and injured 1,500 and the city mortuary was unable to cope with the great number of deaths. On April 19th, a Belfast Telegraph reporter wrote, "Thousands of people were in tears today as the funerals of the air-raid victims passed through the streets of Belfast. It was a sombre and affecting scene. Coffin after coffin, hearse after hearse. They passed in such numbers that one inevitably lost all count and could only stand there in dazed silence, a lump in the throat. Women and children wept unrestrainedly, many for some loved one passing to the last resting place in that grim procession, and many others out of sympathy for those who had been bereaved. Never before had Belfast witnessed the like of it". The fire-raid of 4th - 5th May 1941 witnessed, if anything, an event even more devastating. Attacking from a height of 9,000 - 13,000 feet, the German bombers dropped 200 metric tons of explosives and 96,000 incendiary bombs over two and a half hours. The following night more bombers came attacking the city for four hours and leaving hardly a street in the commercial area without damage.

The story is told of an incident in a shelter during one of the three Belfast raids where Catholic and Protestant people were singing provocative party songs. The Roman Catholics sang "Kevin Barry" and the Protestants sang "The Sash". Then, as the bombs drew nearer, they united in the familiar strains of "Nearer My God To Thee". "T.B.F.", unfortunately, did not come nearer to God in this period of his life. "I had not intended to drift from God", he recalls, "but through wrong company and careless ways, I found myself caught in the grip of evil habits and far from God."

He now launched into hauling stones for the runways at proposed aerodromes. He purchased two diesel lorries, A.E.C.s, registered EMC 147 and EMC 148 from England and hauled stones from quarries to Aghadowey, Cranfield and Ballykelly. In August 1937 Roy McMillan commenced employment with T. B. Thompson in the shop yard, loading the lorries. Tommy Linton was an assistant in the shop from 1937 and was later joined by Ernie Moore in 1941. "T.B.F.'s" brother, Billy, and Johnny Linton, took over the "grocery run" and, at last "T.B.F." was finally, as they say in Ulster, "out on his own".

"T.B.F.'s" lorries got their petrol from Nutt's Garage in Limavady and coming in and out of the place he became very friendly with the proprietor, Mr. R. J. Pattison Nutt. Mr. Nutt had been in the public transport business with buses. He ran a bus service called the "Super Nutt" service from Limavady to Londonderry.

"T.B.F." liked him from the start. The chats by petrol pumps soon led to chats about hauling stones and "T.B.F." suggested that they both go into partnership and trade as "Thompson and Nutt". They leased, together, in time a number of quarries: the first one at Croaghan, half way between Garvagh and Coleraine, another at Ballymulderg outside Magherafelt, and one near Newtownards called The White Spots Quarry from which they hauled stones to the aerodrome at Millisle. They also leased a quarry at Ballyward in County Down to haul stones to Nutt's Corner. This aerodrome would eventually become Northern Ireland's main airport and perhaps only in Northern Ireland could its first major airport be called "Nutt's Corner"! "Thompson and Nutt" also leased a quarry at Annalong from which stones were drawn for the aerodrome at Cranfield. "T.B.F." could be seen driving off on a Friday morning in his Vauxhall 10, registered JI 8608 with a paper bag containing the wages for the men employed at the quarries. Friday was a long day. "T.B.F." has always held a deep affection for his friend, Mr. Nutt. Temperamentally he was a complex man and was given to bouts of withdrawing into himself, but, underlying this trait was a deep reserve of kindness. He was a superb worker.

The war years saw "T.B.F." slide into a very shady world. He began to drink quite heavily, particularly in the border town of Milford, County Donegal, where one of his favourite haunts was James Arbuckle Diamond's Pub. There is no question that smuggling was a way of life for the tens of thousands of people living along the border between Northern Ireland and the Republic of Ireland during the war years. It was not in any way regarded like the smuggling of drugs, for example, is regarded today but it was mostly in the line of half pounds of tea or pounds of sugar and butter smuggled from the Republic and pounds of flour "flowing" the other way. "T.B.F." was not behind his comtemporaries in smuggling lots of sugar and butter and solemnly asserts to this day that he gave most of it away as gifts. The few lorries that he smuggled, though, he kept to himself and they constituted the most serious aspect of his smuggling activities. Lorries were very hard to obtain in Northern Ireland but were available in the Republic of Ireland.

It was illegal to bring them back across the border but "T.B.F." found ways and means of, as he calls it, "jumping the border". He even "jumped" a lovely Chrysler car, registration ZD 2826, and, when the customs men came looking for it, he "jumped" the border back again! There was one outstanding incident where "T.B.F." very nearly. faced the prosecution he deserved. Two of his drivers were caught "jumping the border" with a lorry and one was arrested and allowed out on bail. A customs post man called Kealey was sent to Coleraine to pick out "T.B.F.'s" driver in an identification parade. "T.B.F." and his friends got the five men all of similar size and the driver, in the identification parade, to have similar haircuts, wear the same boilersuits and face the music! Kealey couldn't identify his man!

The case was eventually settled out of court and "T.B.F." paid up. "T.B.F." must have been an extremely popular character around Garvagh in the war years for the women of the district went almost crazy for the silk stockings he brought across the border. They were years of intrigue and heavy drinking bouts and illegality but he now looks back upon them with regret. He calls them "the wasted years". As for the accusation that his future business empire was built from money made from smuggling, the accusation will simply not stand. He was by the 1950's, as we shall see, to face virtual disaster in business and his subsequent rise to business prominence came from acumen, hard work, and the application of moral principles which were to soon invade and change his life. One Sunday evening in 1946 "T.B.F." found himself drinking in "The Marine Arms" in Ballycastle. He returned home to Garvagh and went to bed. The following morning he couldn't rise and became completely stiffened up and had to be carried down stairs. Sent to Miss Bradshaw's Nursing Home in Belfast, he lay for another period, unable to move. At one stage of his illness he received an injection every three hours for ten days. His conscience began to probe him heavily and he knew that he had wandered far in his moral standards from the teaching of his mother and father. He felt ashamed the way he was wasting his life and promised God, in prayer, that if he were restored to health he would be different.

His health returned and to recuperate from the illness, "T.B.F." and his friend Pattison Nutt set off for Egypt, via Malta. It was in the days of King Farouk and the two Ulstermen went up the Nile on a steamer for ten days as far as Aswan and stayed at the Cataract Hotel. They then returned, by a train journey of 600 miles, to Cairo ,when suddenly "T.B.F." fell ill again and the authorities at the Anglo-Irish hospital refused to let him out. As he lay in the three-bed ward he made a decision and what ensued was like a scene from the film "Casablanca"! He signed himself out and caught one of the only planes available at the time out of Cairo to Tunisa and arrived home to Garvagh via Marseille in France. Bouncing back to health, quickly, one of his first business deals on returning to his "feet" was to buy in November 1946 seventy ex-Army vehicles at Toomebridge in County Antrim. He bought them at an auction of ex-Army equipment and had them driven in convoy to Garvagh. They were quite a sight as their drivers tried to negotiate the corner and the turns in the middle of Maghera and they were eventually lined up in Garvagh Main Street. When people were walking to church early on the Sunday morning they were more than surprised to see such a line of Army vehicles in their small town. Some of them actually thought that war had been declared again! Thankfully it wasn't true for peace had come to the United Kingdom and, in fact, peace was soon to come to the life of T.B.F. Thompson in a way he had never imagined. It was to prove to be a peace which passed all understanding.

♦ CHAPTER SIX ♦

"The Power of one"

HOW IMPORTANT IS THE INFLUENCE OF ONE? THE answer is that the influence of one is incalculable. Kellogg minus a farmer equals no cornflakes. If the nail factory closes what good is the hammer factory? Schubert's genius wouldn't have amounted to much if the piano tuner hadn't showed up. An Evelyn Glennie is needed to bring out the true beauty of sound from a xylophone. A cracker maker does better if there's a cheese maker. The most skilful surgeon needs the ambulance driver who delivers the patients. Rogers needed Hammerstein and T.B.F. Thompson needed Edna Burns.

Edna, now Mrs Charlie McKee, was a sincere and dedicated Christian and was deeply worried about "T.B.F.'s" slide into a dissolute and morally ambivalent lifestyle. For years Edna had prayed for him and although she was never his girlfriend, she was part of the circle of his acquaintances and hated to see him waste his life.

One evening in July 1947 Edna invited "T.B.F." to hear a very famous Christian preacher present the Christian Gospel.

The preacher was no ordinary preacher and his name was a household name throughout Northern Ireland. A Presbyterian Minister with a difference, the Rev. William Patteson Nicholson had influenced tens of thousands for Christ. His humour was legendary, his style pithy and direct, his dedication unquestioned.

From shipyard workers to Cambridge University students, who carried him on their shoulders to his train after his Cambridge Mission, he was to become a great friend of "T.B.F's", but, he wasn't high on "T.B.F's" agenda in July 1947.

"T.B.F." wasn't in the slightest bit interested in Nicholson's Evangelistic Mission in Cookstown, County Tyrone, and would have preferred a night's drinking, any time, to attendance at a mission, but, he decided to go.

Interestingly enough the Christian evangelistic service did not touch him. It was Edna who stirred up his spiritual lethargy. "I am no preacher, Tom", said Edna on the way home from the service, "but I'm going to ask you a question. Are you saved?". She then related to "T.B.F." how she and another friend had been to a similar evangelistic service and on the way home her friend had said, "I don't think I'll ever be saved". She hadn't the courage to speak to him and in the following week he died, tragically. Edna's witness went like an arrow into the balloon of emptiness that was cocooning "T.B.F.'s" life. He suddenly saw his life for what it was and began to think of his relationship with God and the state of his soul. For, after all, Christ had said, "What shall it profit a man if he should gain the whole world and lose his own soul?" "T.B.F." very well knew that the answer was "absolutely nothing".

People, of course, often wonder why Christians use the word "saved". It has, for many who hear it, a sectarian ring about it. It smacks to them of an exclusive group of people who look down on everyone else and is viewed as a "Holier-than-thou" word. Non-Christians often strain to follow Christians' words when they express their faith.

Some of the words they use are, as far as they are concerned, religious gobblydegook. Christians think the words they are using to describe a spiritual experience which they have passed through are clear but the phrases are very often foreign to those around them. One of the toughest assignments in life, of course, is to communicate clearly what happened during a time when emotions ran high. Take these actual words of people who tried to summarize their encounters with trouble. The following is a series of actual quotes taken from insurance or accident forms:

"Coming home, I drove into the wrong house and collided with a tree I don't have."

"The other car collided with mine without giving a warning of its intention."

"I thought my window was down, but I found it was up when I put my hand through it."

"I collided with a stationary truck coming the other way."

"A truck backed through my windscreen into my wife's face."

"A pedestrian hit me and went under my car."

"The guy was all over the road; I had to swerve a number of times before I hit him."

"I pulled away from the side of the road, glanced at my mother-in-law, and rolled over the embankment."

"In my attempt to kill a fly, I drove into a telephone pole."

"I had been shopping for plants all day, and was on my way home. As I reached an intersection, a hedge sprang up obscuring my vision. I did not see the other car."

"I had been driving for 40 years when I fell asleep at the wheel and had an accident."

"I was on the way to the doctor's with rear end trouble when my universal joint gave way, causing me to have an accident".

"To avoid hitting the bumper of the car in front, I struck the pedestrian."

"As I approached the intersection, a Stop sign suddenly appeared in a place where no Stop sign had ever appeared before. I was unable to stop in time to avoid the accident."

"My car was legally parked as it backed into the other vehicle."

"An invisible car came out of nowhere, struck my vehicle and vanished."

"I told the police that I was not injured, but removing my hat, I found I had a skull fracture."

"The pedestrian had no idea which direction to go, so I ran over him."

"I was sure the old fellow would never make it to the other side of the road when I struck him."

"I saw the slow-moving, sad-faced old gentleman as he bounced off the bonnet of my car."

"The indirect cause of this accident was a little guy in a small car with a big wife."

"I was thrown from my car as it left the road. I was later found in a ditch by some stray cows."

"The telephone pole was approaching fast. I attempted to swerve out of its path when it struck my front end."

"I was unable to stop in time and my car crashed into the other vehicle. The driver and passenger then left immediately for a vacation with injuries."

There is certainly no doubt that emotions have a way of overwhelming logical thinking and precise communication! Yet the word "saved" that Edna Burns used to challenge "T.B.F." is an extremely important word. The Bible doesn't view the word as a "Holier-than-thou" expression. It views it as a vital word and it couldn't have been better expressed than the way the Apostle

Paul expressed it; "For", he wrote, "by grace are you saved through faith and that not of yourselves, it is the gift of God not of works lest any man should boast". What did he mean about being 'saved'? An illustration might help.

Walking through Burrington Combe, a beautiful spot in Somersetshire, one day, the Vicar of Blagdon, the Rev. Augustus M. Toplady was caught, suddenly, in a storm. The Vicar was in a very exposed place and espied a massive rock beside the road in which he was able to take refuge until the storm abated.

Toplady, while in the cleft, picked up a playing card lying at his feet and wrote upon the back of it the hymn of which it has been said that, "No other English hymn can be named which has laid so broad and firm a grasp upon the English speaking world", beginning,

"Rock of Ages, Cleft for me!
Let me hide myself in Thee".

Walking recently through the beautiful conservation village of Broadhembury, in Devonshire, this author happened to enter the local Parish Church. There in the quintessence of an English Parish Church, he read on the wall the following memorial inscription:

"Rev. Augustus M. Toplady
Vicar 1768 - 1778
Author of the immortal hymn "Rock of Ages"
To whose personal piety, brilliant gifts,
sanctified learning and uncompromising
advocacy of the Gospel of the Sovereign
Grace of God, his writings bear abundant
testimony.
Died 11th August, 1778, in his 38th year.

"For by grace are ye saved through
faith and that not of yourselves,
it is the gift of God not of works
lest any man should boast".
Ephesians 2: 8.

Stirred deeply by what he read, his eyes fell on a memorial plaque to a prominent lady of the district which was placed right beside Toplady's memorial. Part of it read,

"Her long and virtuous life was spent
in the quiet and steady performance
of every righteous and moral duty
in humble hope of immortality".

The stark difference between the two memorials could not have been more obvious. One told of a person who died with the obvious assurance of salvation and the other told of a person who died with the mere hope of it. Was Toplady "Holier-than-thou" in his assurance of salvation? Certainly not! He noted in his immortal hymn that his salvation had nothing to do with the performance of righteous and moral duties. He wrote,

"Nothing in my hand I bring,
Simply to Thy cross I cling;
Naked, come to Thee for dress,
Helpless, look to Thee for grace;
Foul I to the fountain fly,
Wash me, Saviour, or I die."

On that July evening in 1947 "T.B.F." went to his bed and read a little booklet called "God's Way of Salvation" which Edna had given to him. It expounded clearly the truth Toplady had discovered in the 18th century and millions more have discovered in the centuries before and since, the truth that salvation is not by works, commendable though they are, but by faith in Christ alone.

"T.B.F." climbed out of his bed and fell to his knees in prayer, repenting toward God and putting his faith in Jesus Christ as his personal Saviour. No decision he ever took was to affect his life and destiny so deeply.

The whole direction of "T.B.F.'s" life was now turned around, and, instead of merely being an accumulator of wealth, he became one of the most outstanding Christian stewards of wealth in his generation. His philanthropy has become legendary. Untold numbers of people have benefitted. Whether a person is gifted in business like "T.B.F." or gifted in other ways, when Christ comes into their life, those gifts now have very real meaning and can be used to the blessing of others in fresh and new ways. People around them know there is a change and, truth is, even more than people know it. Like the famous Duncan Donaldson, the "Wild Man of Airdrie" who was in prison 88 times for drunkeness, it was not only people who noticed the change in his life when he got converted. On the evening of his conversion to Christ he who had usually kicked his front door open at night, quietly opened his front door and his own dog bit him! Why? The dog thought his master was a stranger!

Northern Ireland was soon to feel the impact of Christian witness through the life of T.B.F. Thompson. His true fortune had just been made and money couldn't buy it for, as his mother had taught him, "The gift of God is eternal life through Jesus Christ our Lord." That gift is without money and without price and is available to everyone.

Kathleen Laughlin as a Nursing Sister in the City and County Hospital, Londonderry about the time of her first date with "T.B.F."

◆ CHAPTER SEVEN ◆

"I'll take you home again, Kathleen"

IMAGINE, IF YOU WOULD, A HUGE STORM IN Mid-Atlantic. Here is a liner plunging her way through huge swells and on board are passengers on their knees crying to God to allow their lives to be spared. They solemnly promise God never to return to America again if they can but make Europe's shore. One of them is a young County Londonderry lass from a family that went back to the 13th century, the Laughlin family.

As it happened the lass had just been to visit her extremely wealthy uncle in the United States who had promised to leave her his entire estate. Irony of ironies, when he died and his lawyers wrote asking the now much older Londonderry lady to come to America and claim her inheritance, she refused. She would not go back on her promise to God made on board the liner at the height of the unforgettable storm.

She did, though, receive £500 which, in those far-off days, was a considerable sum of money and gave it to her son and daughter-in- law, William and Aveline Laughlin to buy a new farm. William and Aveline lived at that time at the Black Falls at Bovevagh in County Londonderry. They bought their new farm at Glack, Tarnakelly, five miles from Limavady and were just delighted at the better living conditions it brought. At Glack eleven children were born to them, six girls and five boys.

As Tolstoy said, "All happy families resemble one another, each unhappy family is unhappy in its own way". "You would not have got any family happier than we were", said Lena, one of the six girls born into the Laughlin home at Glack. William was a great fiddler and on wet days when his family couldn't dig potatoes or gather the harvest in, he would call on them and his neighbour's families to come into his big farm kitchen. He got them dancing like nobody's business. His little slip of a wife was in there with the best of them; Aveline was never more than seven stone in weight! She did all the farm work, including the milking, and raised her eleven children without ever hearing of Rosemary Conley, or, Shirley Conran either!

Off the fourteen Laughlins, including grandmother, would go to church on Sundays in their trap with their lovely black thoroughbred horse high-stepping his way through Tarnakelly. Kathleen's elder sister, Lena, interviewed for this book just a few weeks before her sad death in December, 1994, recalled the fun they had all had together those seventy years previous. There was not much money around and their Christmases were not memorable for material gifts. Yet they had the best of gifts in the love and time given to them by their parents. In our modern day of satellites and multi TV channels and of video games bringing "virtual reality", few children have to draw on their own imagination to while away their childhood hours. Their demands for material things, brought on particularly under the pressure of television advertising can often be frightening. Yet, parents need to remember that money and material things are not the best gifts they can give to make childhood days memorable.

"It is not hard to make a child's heart glad,
Often a little thing will please, will ease,
A tear-filled afternoon,
A walk, a ride across the park,
A story read, a small suprise,
A "Let's pretend,"
Will make their childhood glad.

Father busy in your office, plush,
Rushing around so much, you cannot touch,
Your children's heart that way,
Oh! It may buy them food or toys,
But you must give them time,
Your time, if you would ever say,
"I've made their childhood glad."

Mother, who daily makes the mould,
In those first years, edged by fears,
Fears of how they'll fare,
Make yours the encouraging word,
And hold their love, even when they rebel,
Always care, always care,
And you'll make their childhood glad.

Then, when they've left your patient care,
Leaving the nest, and the rest,
To make their own,
When you are old and their childhood's gone,
Far from your grasp and reach,
They'll say of you to children of their own,
"They made my childhood glad."

William and Aveline certainly made their children's lives truly happy. One of their daughters, Kathleen, turned out to be an outstanding nurse. One of Kathleen's best friends in childhood was a doctor's daughter called Nora Matson. Her father ran a clinic in the area every Thursday for poor people and did not charge them a penny for his services. For ordinary folk he charged only one pound each. Nora, who was later to become Matron of the City and County Hospital in Londonderry, deeply influenced Kathleen to follow her into nursing.

Kathleen became a very dedicated nurse and surgeons used to ask for her when dealing with special cases because of her abilities. She had, of course, hundreds of patients to look after including the father of the famous tenor singer, Joseph Locke.

One evening in July, 1947 Kathleen Laughlin had a very rude awakening from sleep. She had been on night duty and was sleeping soundly when she found herself being shaken by her friend Nora Matson. A young man had arrived in Londonderry to find his date was ill and Nora asked Kathleen to go on a blind date. Even Cilla Black could not have found a more reluctant candidate; Kathleen was angry at being awakened and went reluctantly. She hardly spoke a word all night.

The young man was, of course, the "Bee Charmer" and he had to produce all the charm he possessed that evening. Six months later, though, "T.B.F." bought Kathleen an engagement ring in Dublin and they were married in his own family home by special licence on June 9th, 1948. After their wedding they honeymooned at the Grand Hotel in Greystones and then toured Ireland. They drove as far as Cork and up through Galway and Connemara as far as Westport and on to Sligo, Donegal town and back to Thompson's Corner in Garvagh. It all took one week.

Their first years together were certainly in restricted circumstances with only three bedrooms and a kitchen-dinette shared with T.B.F.'s father and Auntie Dolly. When eventually on 25th

August 1955, "T.B.F." and Kathleen moved into "Heathlands", the house "T.B.F." had built on the outskirts of Garvagh, "T.B.F." found that he was miserable for at least two years. Why? Because he so missed living in the town!

In fact he held on to his rooms at Thompson's Corner for two to three years because he really thought he would go back. We are talking, of course, of only moving half a mile away from the family home! He actually went back into town on the night he moved into his beautiful new home to see his father and wept. "T.B.F." very nearly literally fulfilled the words of the song, "I'll take you home again, Kathleen"!

"T.B.F.'s" miserable feelings on moving half a mile from the centre of the town of Garvagh did not reflect, however, the state of his marriage. His marriage was to prove one of the most stable factors in his life. His wife loved antiques, though, and was to become known far and wide across Northern Ireland for her bidding skills at auctions. When she set her mind on something she was a formidable bidder. "You're not having it", she said once to a Minister who desperately wanted a certain antique at an auction. Kathleen outbid him but imagine his surprise when she paid the bill and gave him the antique, for free. That was Kathleen.

"T.B.F." and Kathleen never had any children, yet, it was never a cause for bitterness between them. In fact it was a subject very seldom discussed and they took the situation as being God's will for them and got on with their lives. In days when the psychiatrist's couch is overloaded with stressed-out people, such thinking is rare but that is the way "T.B.F." and Kathleen felt and thought.

Their relationship was uncomplicated and very happy and that's a fact. Kathleen couldn't have balanced an account book any more than climbed Everest and her husband was to balance accounts containing millions but one complemented the other. Although Kathleen could not have balanced an account book she was a great homemaker and, interestingly, an outstandingly gifted flower arranger. Many were the comments passed on the beautiful arrangements she presented at various functions at "Heathlands" over the years. Opposites attract and these opposites stayed attracted. Not many "tycoon couples" have such a track record in marriage. The complicated lifestyles of people in T.V. soap operas like "Dallas" or "Dynasty" was not the lifestyle of this couple. It seems incredible that a certain jeweller's shop recently had a sign in the window which read, "We rent wedding rings". "T.B.F." and Kathleen never considered selling theirs.

♦ CHAPTER EIGHT ♦

"The school of Hard Knocks"

IN 1947 AN INTERESTING OPPORTUNITY AROSE FOR the "Thompson-Nutt" Partnership. Samuel Wright of Strabane approached the partnership for advice regarding the sale of his business, the Strabane Service Station. He wished to emigrate to South Africa and the partnership not only gave him advice, they purchased his business in November 1947. A young man called R. J. Gillanders was at that time working for Mr. Wright and now started to work for the new owners. Affectionately known as Bertie, R. J. Gillanders was, without question, to become the closest business colleague "T.B.F." ever had through all of his long business life in Northern Ireland.

In November 1947, though, Bertie was earning two pounds ten shillings a week at the Strabane Service Station. Travelling in a car one day "T.B.F." turned to Bertie and suggested an increase in salary. He asked Bertie what he would like and Bertie, drawing breath, decided he would go the whole hog and ask for the princely sum of five pounds a week. "T.B.F." recalls to this day that Pattison Nutt suddenly turned round on Bertie and said, "Would four pounds not do you, boy?". To his eternal credit "T.B.F." would have none of this compromise and Bertie got his request!

It is hard for this generation in Northern Ireland to understand how very poor families were just after the war in comparison to today's standards. Bertie's father came from a background where he went to school in his bare feet in the summertime. With the other children, in winter, he took a piece of turf in his schoolbag along with his books to keep the schoolhouse fire burning.

Bertie Gillanders had a trait in him which was right in sync with "T.B.F."; he loved cars and speed. As they say in Northern Ireland, from the time he was "knee-high to a grasshopper" he was driving. When applying for a driving licence he belied his age and slipped through the net. He was a member of the auxiliary fire service in Strabane and was driving fire engines at the age of 14! In fact the day he was fourteen he had left school, and, like "T.B.F." before him, he simply could not wait to get away from the restricting world of academia! When eventually he did begin to work for the Thompson-Nutt partnership, his health, unfortunately, broke down. He experienced a very severe stomach haemorrhage and was in hospital for quite some time. When he recovered he decided to move out into business on his own.

"T.B.F.'s" partnership with Pattison Nutt, though, was running into problems and "T.B.F." felt that in light of the problems it would be better to sever the connection at the earliest, most convenient moment, and, in the most amicable manner. It took more than two years to dissolve the partnership which involved two businesses, namely the Central Motor Company in Garvagh and the Strabane Service Station. Major Jack Baxter of the solicitors, Wray and Baxter, Coleraine advised that both businesses be set up for sale at an auction. The first was held in Garvagh with Mr. Jim Watters of Milford as the auctioneer. There were only two bidders, Thompson and Nutt and "T.B.F." let his friend Pattison Nutt have the the Central Motor Company. When the Strabane Service Station came up for auction, "T.B.F." bid for it and didn't get it but, in fact, bought it later from the people who did!

During all of this time Bertie Gillanders had been buying cars in the Republic and bringing them into Northern Ireland and would, from time to time, go down to Garvagh when he had a customer and buy lorries from "T.B.F." They became very friendly and on buying the Strabane Service Station for himself, "T.B.F." put Bertie in as the manager. For the next fifty years Bertie was to be the engineering brain behind "T.B.F.'s" business expansion. He was to be, if you like, the Itzhak Stern of the operation and "T.B.F." was to be, as Oscar Schindler would have put it, the expert on "presentation". A small farm which had belonged to the Thompson-Nutt partnership at Strabane was sold to Dr. Brown, a local G.P. at this time.

"T.B.F." was now in a position to expand, though, at this point, he made one of the biggest mistakes of his life which was to teach him some very salutory lessons. He had been involved in the Toomebridge area hauling sand and lime bricks for the Northern Sand and Brick Company, and he purchased 22 lorries to do the haulage. He bought a brick company in Campsie, Londonderry, and named it The Derry Brickworks Ltd. He lacked experience, couldn't really afford it, and ran not so much into a brick company as into a brick wall called Union trouble. The men in the Union demanded more money and "T.B.F." reckoned it an unfair demand as he was paying the same rate as other brick companies, even though his brickworks was losing money, weekly. The aggro grew and grew and "T.B.F." got sick of it all and one day decided to act. A favourite maxim of his good friend Jack Baxter was, "Never draw a gun unless you are going to shoot," so "T.B.F." drew his "gun" and "shot"!

A meeting had been arranged with the Union leader and a "man from the Ministry" at the Melville Hotel in Londonderry but "T.B.F." went to the brickworks, first. He told the men that if they did not go back to work he was going to close the works down for good. The men refused, "T.B.F." paid them their week's wages and told them to let the kiln fires go out. He then went to meet the Union leader at the Melville Hotel and told him of his decision. He eventually sold the land and its buildings, after seven years, to the Government.

What did he learn from this experience? He learnt that management is all important in running any business. Just as any church gets a name for being unfriendly if it has an unfriendly steward on its front door, so any business is judged by the personnel who manage it. No matter how much money is poured into a business, if there are not capable people managing the business, then the whole thing will founder. His good friend, Major Jack Baxter had advised him many times, "Delegate or die - but you must be careful who you delegate to." "T.B.F.'s" golden rule from the time of the brickworks disaster onwards became, "If you haven't got good management, then get it fast!". He also learned from Jack Baxter the important fact that if you want to have any major influence in a Company, being a minority share holder is not a good launching pad to that influence.

He also learnt that to buy a company without potential is a disaster. He should have sent in an analyst to check out the clay for his bricks and to work out the potential for its development but he failed to do so. The Derry Brickworks was quite a blister for "T.B.F." but he put it down to experience and the blister healed.

In the same year he purchased an additional 5 new AEC tipper lorries with 9.6 diesel engines at £2,000 each to expand his haulage business. "T.B.F." also bought a company at this time from James Pollock in Coleraine and started shipping potatoes. He also acquired a company called King and Alexander, a coachworks, and formed a new company called Thompson Coach and Motor Works to service his own lorries in Coleraine. He bought the West Bay View Hotel in Portrush, knives, forks, spoons; the lot! His friend Jim Watters was a partner in the hotel for a while but pulled out, eventually. "T.B.F." owned the 53 roomed hotel from 1951 - 1957 and it did a roaring trade with commercial travellers and holiday makers.

There are many other tales that could be told about the Thompson years at the West Bay View; it was not altogether a "Fawlty Towers" but what happened to the Fawlty's in fiction was not far off the mark in reality in the day-to-day running of the Portrush Hotel. There were problems with chefs and Bertie Gillanders recalls a chef getting up and leaving the West Bay View and when "T.B.F." discovered he was gone and in Dublin, Bertie was dispatched to fetch him from Dublin, some 200 miles distant, and bring him back to keep the immediate hotel residents fed and watered!

There was one occasion on the last day of May, when a chef and a manageress walked out on "T.B.F.". The next day a big church excursion, the first one of the year, had booked into the West Bay View for their meals. The "ship" was now without a captain and a chief engineer and a full-scale emergency was on hand, and, the rocks were looming! "T.B.F." called in Kathleen and the people who worked at his Garvagh headquarters (including their wives!) and they were dispatched to the kitchen and the dining room of the West Bay View Hotel and were set to work. They did such a job for the church excursion that the church booked the hotel for the same occasion for the following year! They thought that Kathleen was the manageress and she got a tip when they were leaving!

But, truth is, T.B.F. Thompson was no Billy Hastings. He admits it freely and was eventually glad to leave hostelry for wider business activity. Already involved in hauling sand, he decided, with H.A.C. Catherwood and Sons Ltd., to pump sand from the shores of Lough Neagh with 6 inch Wynne pumps. This company was known as the "Thompson Sand and Gravel Company". On top of all this he began building his new home, "Heathlands" on the edge of Garvagh.

"Heathlands" almost landed "T.B.F." in court. In building the house he exceeded in size the building restrictions set by the Government. He was officially summoned for breaching of building regulations and the case "Ministry of Finance -v- T.B.F. Thompson" was set. It was a very serious matter. However, just as the case came up the Government restrictions came off and "T.B.F." escaped prosecution.

Things were not going very well, in general, though. There was a huge drain on "T.B.F.'s" capital and he was beginning to slip in business. One night in 1952 he broke down in tears before his wife Kathleen and reckoned he was finished. Tom's father commented that he reckoned his son was "going too fast" and, at this time, he certainly was. Kathleen had always said she would gladly put on her nursing cap and apron again, if necessary, but, it did not prove to be necessary.

One day in 1954 "T.B.F.", Bertie Gillanders, Jack Baxter and the Bank Manager of the Kilrea Northern Bank, James Boyd, set off on a very important journey to Belfast. The Northern Bank were considering reducing "T.B.F.'s" facility for the first and only time in his life. The facility, or overdraft, was set at a limit of £15,000 and the bank wanted to pull him back to £10,000. The three men entered the Head Office of the Northern Bank to face J.E. Ford, the Chairman and Thomas Dunne, the Senior Managing Director. "T.B.F." was not looking forward to the encounter but the Kilrea Bank Manager decided to go for it.

He emphasized that "T.B.F." simply could not work on an overdraft of £10,000 and asked that his £15,000 overdraft be increased to £20,000! He told the bank's Chairman and Senior Managing Director that he hadn't a qualm about "T.B.F.'s" ability to pay back. To "T.B.F's" lifetime amazement the bank gave him the facility. He returned to Garvagh that night, in his own words "as though I owned Belfast".

76

*Part of the unique, four day Commercial Vehicle Show at TBF Thompson (Belfast)
Ltd at Ravenhill Road, December 4th-7th 1963: the largest of its kind ever seen in
Ireland up until that time.*

*Captain Terence O'Neill, Prime Minister of Northern Ireland, with
"T.B.F." at the opening of the new extension to TBF Thompson
(Garvagh) Ltd in May 1966.*

◆ CHAPTER NINE ◆

"Mr. Potter makes a Call"

THE LAST DAY OF JANUARY 1953 WAS A SATURDAY
and it dawned cold and blustery with the wind gusting up to 60
m.p.h. and increasing steadily. As the day lengthened, showers
of sleet and snow reduced visibility to a few yards, making life
difficult for the coastguards on watch along the coastlines of
Scotland and Northern Ireland. It was to be a day they would
never forget.

The Scottish coastline of Galloway was taking a powerful
pounding when the 2,700 ton Ferry, the PRINCESS VICTO-
RIA, nosed her way out of Lough Ryan under the command of
Captain James Ferguson, setting course for Larne, Northern
Ireland. There was a howling gale and a fearful rolling sea that
made the PRINCESS VICTORIA pitch and roll violently. Not
long after the ship passed Milleur Buoy, disaster struck. A
powerful wave hit the steel hinged doors at the stern of the ship
leaving them buckled and mis-shapen and the sea flooded into
the car deck. Valiant efforts were made to close the doors but the

sea kept on rushing in solidly. The Captain attempted a manoeuvre to take his ship stern-first into the shelter of Lough Ryan but it proved impossible. Captain Ferguson then tried to head for the safety of the Northern Ireland coast, radioing for help.

Lifeboats rushed to the aid of the PRINCESS VICTORIA and the Destroyer H.M.S. CONTEST set out immediately from Rothesay but due to many complications and the vile conditions, including waves fifty feet high, the ship was hard to locate. David Broadfoot, the Radio Officer, sent out 54 distress signals in four and a half hours. One of the very last messages received was "S.O.S. Endeavouring to hold on but ship on beam end. Can see Irish coast". The PRINCESS VICTORIA heeled over and foundered in 45 fathoms of water, about five miles east of the Copeland Islands at the entrance to Belfast Lough.

One hundred and twenty-eight lives were lost in the sinking of the PRINCESS VICTORIA, including the Deputy Prime Minister of Northern Ireland, Major Maynard Sinclair. Captain Ferguson went down with his ship, in the tradition of the sea, and was last seen holding on to the railings and saluting as his ship finally plunged to the depths of the North Channel. The disaster remains the worst sea tragedy in the North Channel and for the generation that lived through the disaster, it remained much like the experience of the generation that lived through the assassination of President Kennedy; people remembered where they were when they first heard news of it.

"T.B.F." remembers that he was in Strabane on the day the PRINCESS VICTORIA foundered. He had taken Hugh and Mary Maybin to see his Service Station and motor business in Strabane and they liked it. He sold the business to Hugh Maybin and his right-hand man, Bertie Gillanders, stayed for three months to help Hugh at the commencement of his ownership. Then Bertie started to work with "T.B.F." full time at Garvagh. He worked a 60 hour week, Tuesdays and Thursdays to

9.30 p.m. and had to often go to England to buy lorries for his boss. He would buy good used trucks, bring them back, shorten their chassis and then turn them into "tippers". Tippers from Garvagh were gold-dust in Northern Ireland at that time to anyone in the haulage industry.

An interesting arrangement arose in those days between Bertie and "T.B.F." Bertie and his wife Martha lived very happily in Strabane and had no wish to move from their comfortable home. They were to have five children, four girls and one boy. Having in-laws who were more than happy to babysit, Bertie decided to live with "T.B.F." and Kathleen at "Heathlands" from Monday to Saturday lunch time. The arrangement lasted for nine years! The longsuffering Martha was happy to keep the home fires burning and on the occasions when labour pains overwhelmed her, she simply rang for a taxi and went off to have her babies at the hospital! The marriage has survived for 43 years and the Garvagh-T.B.F. Thompson priority in no way undermined it! Bertie speaks with great affection of the way Tom and Kathleen looked after him. They treated him like a son and Bertie recalls vividly the nights before a roaring fire when they discussed business and expansion.

Little did they think they were to rise together to become major players in the commerical and business life of the Province. Many were the nights when Tom and Bertie would be trying to sew up a deal with customers and by 11 p.m. there was no deal on the table. "T.B.F." would get on the phone to Kathleen and ask for a snack for the customers who might have a long journey ahead of them. The bacon and eggs would be consumed at 12 midnight and, almost inevitably, the deal was done before the customers took their journey home.

"T.B.F." had suffered a real blow when Thompson-Reid took the Ferguson tractor franchise away from the Strabane

Service Station just after he had taken it over, but, he now made a determined bid to obtain the Hillman car franchise. He didn't have much money to fall back on, but, he proved to Charles Eyre-Mansell of A.S. Baird's in Belfast that he could sell cars as well as he had eggs! He got the Hillman franchise and soon they gave him the Rootes Group franchise for commerical vehicles, including the famous Commer and Karrier vehicles. The two stroke Commer was a best seller and "T.B.F." put on an extension to his premises and opened two nights a week, to 9.30 p.m. for sales.

By 1958 the business had already snowballed and Major Baxter advised "T.B.F." to become a Limited Company. When he applied he found his company could not be named The Thompson Motor Company Ltd. because someone on the mainland already had registered their company in that name. Major Baxter then advised that he register as "T.B.F. Thompson (Garvagh) Ltd." and the Company's Office sanctioned the name. The Company Chairman and the Managing Director was "T.B.F." himself, with Kathleen and Bertie Gillanders as Directors. Major Jack Baxter was appointed Company Secretary, and he proved to be a tremendous help throughout the years as he was not only a solicitor but had an accountant's brain as well.

In 1959 "T.B.F." bought his first premises in Belfast. It was a petrol station at the corner of the Lisburn Road and Marlborough Park and, again, he laid out his plans for expansion and development. Like Henry Ford before him he always had a great belief in having someone make a model of his plans and the model for his Lisburn Road building was, again, innovative and full of promise. Again, though, his plans were thwarted as they were turned down by the City Planners who did not want a heavy vehicle centre on the Lisburn Road. Their word was, "Cars, yes, lorries, no" and "T.B.F." was deeply disappointed as he was very keen to get going in the commercial vehicle business in Belfast.

For the Quakers in the area, though, "T.B.F.'s" appearance in the Lisburn Road area proved to be a literal God-send. They were looking for ground on which to build one of their meeting-houses and when they approached Tom about some further ground he owned in the area, he said they could have it. "How much?", they asked. "For nothing!", he replied. George Fox himself, their founding father, could not have been more pleased. Quakers were first named because when in a Law Court at Derby, where George Fox was being tried, he warned the Judge to "tremble at the Word of the Lord" and the Judge called Fox and his followers Quakers on the spot! Their first name was meant to be a jibe but they have long calmly accepted their nick-name.

The Society of Friends, as they are properly known, are greatly respected across the world and especially in Northern Ireland for their sterling work with the families of men and women who are serving prison sentences. In the Lisburn Road area of Belfast T.B.F. Thompson is always looked upon as a direct answer to prayer amongst the Society of Friends!

There is no question that things do come to those who wait, but "T.B.F." was not finding it easy to wait for an opening in Belfast. He long wondered where his break would come from. It came one Monday evening in 1961 in a call from a Mr. Potter.

J. A. Potter was the Leyland distributor for Northern Ireland, based on Belfast's Ravenhill Road. He was a Protestant married to a Jewess, which must have made an interesting marriage in a Northern Ireland context. Recently on television a famous Northern Ireland Jewish actor told how, as a little boy at school, he was asked by his pals as to his religion. He replied that he was a Jew. "Are you", they asked in all seriousness, "A Protestant Jew or a Catholic Jew?". Such a question could probably only be seriously posed in Northern Ireland! Such questions, though, Joe and Jenny Potter passed off with a smile.

Joe Potter's father had been a blacksmith on the Donegall Road and his son by dint of hard work and flare, rose to high prominence in the commerical vehicle business. One of his former storeboys, James Stewart, O.B.E., speaks of having to clean Joe's office each morning and empty his ashtrays. He recalls that as a sixteen and a half year old lad part of his duties involved buying Joe's "Capstan full-strength" cigarettes, daily. James, Potter's storeboy, was later to become a very popular Lord Mayor of Belfast.

Joe Potter lived on the Antrim Road and his phonecall to "T.B.F." was to bring the break he needed. "I'm not feeling too well", he said, "And I've decided to sell the business and thought you would be the most likely man to be interested in buying it". "T.B.F.'s" door to Belfast was open and by the Wednesday of the next week the deal was done, he bought Potter's assets, property and stock and changed the name to T.B.F. Thompson (Belfast) Ltd. It was one of the major turning points of his business life. He was now appointed the main distributor for Leyland, Albion, Scammel and Ford Commercial vehicles for Northern Ireland based at Ravenhill Road. He was poised to "take off" and "take off" he did. In one famous commercial vehicle show at the Ravenhill Road in 1963 he sold several hundred thousand pounds worth of vehicles at one stroke. A further show in 1964 had a huge response.

All of this expansion brought a very public pat on the back for "T.B.F." and his colleagues one Wednesday in May, 1966. The scene was the opening of new extended workshops and offices for T. B. F. Thompson (Garvagh) Ltd. A band of the

Royal Ulster Constabulary played for one hour before the ceremony in the forecourt of the premises and Captain Terence O'Neill, Prime Minister of Northern Ireland, performed the opening ceremony.

He said he was always encouraged by evidence of local enterprise in Ulster and was particularly delighted when the result was prosperity for a small town like Garvagh. He continued:

"Since this firm began business in Garvagh in 1953 the staff has grown from 12 to more than 70 and the workshops from under 3,000 sq. feet to more than 50,000. It says a great deal for the kind of people who work here that such dramatic development has taken place. I am sure that with such energetic management a limit of the firm's expansion here by no means has been reached. I am told that a further 5 acres of land adjacent to the present site has been acquired. I doubt if this means that Thompson's is diversifying into the farming business!"

Captain O'Neill went on to say that specialised transportation was of great importance in Northern Ireland as a massive five year construction programme was underway. "Industrialists today have some highly specialised requirements", he said, "and in providing custom-built body-work and equipment for commercial vehicles, this firm is providing a very important service".

Referring to the special four day show of commerical vehicles which opened after the ceremony, the Prime Minister said it would be the largest ever staged by a single company in the British Isles. He felt it was a remarkable "first" for Garvagh. He also referred to the ten semi-detached houses which the company had provided for its key workers beside the workshops and said that he was glad to learn that the Coleraine Rural Council would be embarking on another scheme to house further workers. He concluded, "Altogether this is a most impressive development and a very great credit to all concerned. Mr. Thompson himself has had a long connection with Garvagh and it must be of tremendous satisfaction to him to see the results of his efforts for the local community. An expansion on this scale is a gesture of confidence in Ulster. I am sure it will be amply repaid in increased business over the years".

Mr. William Morgan, who was then the Minister of Health and Social Services in the Northern Ireland government, was also present at the opening ceremony and "T.B.F." asked him to accept a twelve seater minibus for the Cripples Institute as a token of appreciation for all the encouragement and help he had received from everyone.

This minibus was in fact the second the firm had donated to local charities and was the seed-bed for a lot more work for charity that was to grow in the coming years in all "T.B.F.'s" enterprises.

"T.B.F." had now moved up on to a very public platform. In 1965 he was honoured to accept the position of being a Justice of the Peace. In his business life he now found that success bred success. The wide publicity that his work was now receiving did not go unnoticed. For most people in Northern Ireland, Garvagh and Rocester - a little town in the West of England - would, in 1966, have appeared to have very little in common. But tiny Garvagh with its population of under one thousand was to emerge as Rocester's best ally in the coming years in the fight against economic depression. Rocester is the headquarters of the giant international construction plant manufacturers, J.C.B., and its founder J. C. Bamford soon heard of the dynamic growth of the T.B.F. Thompson Group. He approached "T.B.F." to see if he would take on the J.C.B. franchise for Northern Ireland.

At that time "T.B.F." was very close to Charles Hurst Ltd., an old established firm in Northern Ireland, founded in 1911. He was close to Charles Hurst's son, Toby, whom he trusted implicitly. Agents for Rover cars and A.E.C. commerical vehicles, they did "T.B.F.'s" servicing work.

One of their Managing Directors was a man called Charlie Stewart, who was to be with the company for 53 years. "T.B.F." used to meet him often for a chat and coffee and mentioned that J.C.B. had approached him for a franchise. To his surprise Charlie Stewart offered to buy T.B.F. Thompson (Belfast) Ltd!

"T.B.F." agreed, and it was, of course, the draughts-player in him that came out during this period of his life. As a lad, spending hours at a draughts-board, he never minded losing a few men if he could gain a king. In 1966 he had gained that king in the J.C.B. franchise and he now turned the full powers of his concentration to expansion in the rubber-tyred excavator business. He soon reached the stage with J.C.B. where one order alone was worth £2,000,000.

"T.B.F.", Kathleen and Mr. and Mrs. J. C. Bamford get airborne at Garvagh on their way to the opening ceremony of the new Belfast depot on 27th November, 1969.

From left: J. C. Bamford, Kathleen, Mrs. Bamford and "T.B.F." arrive at the opening ceremony of the new Belfast depot.

The Prime Minister of Northern Ireland, Major Chichester-Clark, opens the new Belfast depot.

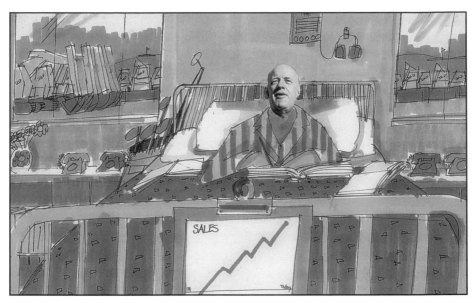

"T.B.F." recovers in the Perth Royal Infirmary in 1972 and receives "Get Well" greetings from J. C. Bamford and his team.

At the R. J. Maxwell & Son quarry site at Bushmills Road, Coleraine.

88

Get-together at "Heathlands" 4th May, 1972, in recognition of the long service of Bobby Brown, Willie Watson, Dora Hegarty and Roy McMillan (seated). All four received back-dated pensions for 30 years. Mr R. J. Gillanders is at the extreme left, back row and Mrs. Martha Gillanders is to Kathleen Thompson's left.

Pictured on the occasion of the presentation of gold watches for long service in 1972.
Left to right: Mr. William Watson, Mrs. Rita Watson, "T.B.F.", Miss Dora Hegarty, Mr. Bobby Brown,
Mrs. Mary-Ann Brown, Mr. Roy McMillan, Mrs. Hessie McMillan and Mr. R. J. Gillanders.

"T.B.F." and Kathleen together at a Civic function.

♦ CHAPTER TEN ♦

"From Nutt's to Bolton's"

GARVAGH WAS SOON THE SCENE OF A "YELLOW and black invasion". No, they weren't bees, but the "bee-charmer" was selling so many yellow and black painted J.C.B. excavators that they came down the road from Belfast to Garvagh likes bees on a summer's day. Nobody was more pleased to see the loaders unloading the excavators than J.C. Bamford himself.

"T.B.F." was now J. C. Bamford's sole representative in Northern Ireland and Co.Donegal and sales were simply phenomenal. Even the second hand trade in excavators was second to none, backed up by a huge spare-part department in Garvagh.

The J.C.B. company put two aircraft at the disposal of its distributors and "T.B.F." made good use of this facility. He used a J.C.B. aircraft regularly to fly at least eight customers at a time to the J.C.B. headquarters at Rocester near Utoxeter in Staffordshire. His customers were then shown around the J.C.B. headquarters and watched demonstrations of the versatility of J.C.B. machinery. It used to be said in fun that "T.B.F." got more plant machinery orders in the air on the way home than he did on the ground!

In the June of 1968 a young accountant arrived at Garvagh to do an audit of "T.B.F." Thompson (Garvagh) Ltd. He managed to do the audit speedily and "T.B.F." was very impressed with his efficiency. His name was Andrew Magowan and when he later saw an advertisement in the press for the position of Assistant Accountant with T.B.F. Thompson (Garvagh) Ltd., he immediately applied for it. The position carried company housing and Andrew and his fiancee, Betty, planned to get married in September 1969. He got the job and they brought their marriage forward to March. Andrew began work on April 1st, 1969 and recalls "T.B.F's" generosity in giving him a rise in pay on June 1st along with all the other annual rises obtained by employees of the company.

Andrew recalls how Tom and Kathleen used to take a walk on Sunday afternoons and on one particular day walked past his home. Kathleen saw what Andrew describes as his "rickety old car" and commented, "With all the cars about Garvagh, Tom, could you not give that man a company car?" Andrew got his car. He became Chief Accountant of the company in 1973 and a Director in 1974. He still fondly remembers the day when at the end of one Balmoral Show week, where "T.B.F." had a Stand (see photograph) he banked £1,000,000 for the company on the last day of the financial year. A lot of J.C.Bs. had moved out across Northern Ireland in that week, for sure!

So great was the expansion that "T.B.F." started to think about opening up a centre again in Belfast. It is complicated, but, it's true; he had sold T.B.F. Thompson (Belfast) Ltd. to Charles Hurst Ltd., now he decided to open up another T.B.F. Thompson (Belfast) Ltd., but this time in another property bought off (who else?) Charles Hurst Ltd.! The centre was at

520 Shore Road, situated on the main arterial road to Belfast
city centre and within close proximity to the M2 motorway.
Hire service and spare parts would now be more easily available
to J.C.B. owners throughout County Down, County Armagh
and County Antrim.

It was, to say the least, a grand opening. "T.B.F.", J. C.
Bamford and their wives along with Tony Bamford travelled by
helicopter from Garvagh to the Shore Road for the official
opening of the new Belfast depot on Thursday, 27th November,
1969. The official opening ceremony was performed by the
then Prime Minister of Northern Ireland, Major The Right
Honourable James Chichester-Clark. There is no doubt that
"Wee Johnny Funny" would have loved it! J.C. Bamford's
speech on the occasion is worth recording. He said: "When I
first heard from my very close friend, T. B.F. Thompson, that
he was opening a new branch in Belfast, I was delighted.

First, because the increase in business in Northern Ireland
has necessitated extra space and secondly, because I am sure it
will be an advantage to have a depot in the capital city.

In the relatively short time J.C.B. and T. B. F. Thompson
organisations have been associated, a tremendously successful
partnership has developed. This has been beneficial to everyone concerned. Over this eventful period my admiration for the
T. B. F. Thompson organisation has grown. I admire the
progress that has been made through the dynamic leadership
and go-ahead management, plus the drive and integrity of the
staff. Spacious showrooms and workshops, ample facilities for
stocking spare parts and radio control cars and vans serve to
outline my statement.

T. B. F. Thompson and I have often spoken about, and agree
that, basically, only two people matter in this business - the

customer who has complete confidence in the equipment, and the man who operates that equipment. It is not enough to simply provide a sales service. The customer expects an after-sales service and when he deals with T.B.F. Thompson, he gets one - second to none. This makes the owner and operator satisfied customers.

The fact that J.C.B. machines are the market leaders in Ulster is partly due to the fact that J.C.B. equipment is the best, and partly due to the tremendously high quality and representation in Ulster by the T. B. F. Thompson Group. The two go hand in hand and a highly successful partnership has been the outcome."

The draughts player in "T.B.F.", though, was not dormant. He knew it was a very dangerous thing for anyone in business to be completely dependent on a single manufacturer. Franchises can be taken away and he needed to be able to fall back on a few "kings" of his own. A fall-back "king" on the draughtsboard of "T.B.F.'s" business life came in a remarkable way. Life, of course, doesn't swing so much on big events as little ones.

Maxwell, the famous Northern Ireland road building firm, was established by the Ulsterman Robert Maxwell at the turn of the century. Maxwell laid the first coated macadam in Northern Ireland in Kerr Street, Portrush around 1920. The firm enjoyed a consistently high reputation for the supply of high quality aggregates and excellent workmanship. First established in Bushtown, Coleraine, Robert Maxwell transferred his plant to Spital Hill in 1936. Constantly innovative, Howard Maxwell, son of the founder, became the first operator in Ireland to use a mechanical paver for laying macadam. Sadly, Howard died at the early age of only 46 and the family business was taken over by W. M. Bolton, the Civil Engineering company. The new company was named "R. J. Maxwell & Son, Ltd."

One Saturday in June 1971, W. M. Bolton happened to come over to check out "T.B.F.'s" driveway at "Heathlands" in preparation for tarring it. As he walked around the grounds he chanced a remark which set "T.B.F." on the way to a "king" to fall back upon if necessary. Willie said, casually, "Tom, if you bought Maxwell's you could do this job yourself!". The remark put Tom into top gear. He never dreamt that Willie Bolton wanted to sell. On the following Monday "T.B.F." bought the Maxwell outfit including the shares of the company.

Soon "T.B.F." was approached by Willie Bolton to see if he would be interested in taking over his own company, W.M. Bolton Ltd. This was, again, a major undertaking and caused "T.B.F." a fair amount of strategic thinking.

When faced with any major decision "T.B.F." has always asked himself a vital question: "What is the worst thing that could happen here?"

Regarding a take-over of Bolton's, he was convinced that it wouldn't put him out of business. "T.B.F." reckoned that he needed his fall-back and with Bolton's came Craigmore Quarries, Kilrea Station and the biggest stone crusher of its kind in Europe, a 36B Pegson Telsmith. With the company came a team whose expertise had introduced asphalt to Northern Ireland and which had pioneered the way for most of today's quarries in Northern Ireland to produce and lay the asphalt surfaces which are so necessary for today's traffic volume.

They had under their outstanding Contract Director, W. J. Telford, gained huge experience in many of Northern Ireland's main roads including the A57 from Ballyclare to Templepatrick, the Ballyclare by-pass, the T7 between Ballymena and Antrim, the 3 mile ring-road at Coleraine, the Glenshane Pass and had even constructed the massive West Bay seawall at Portrush.

When "T.B.F.'s" secretary, Betty Kelly, headed down to Coleraine in her Morris 1100, she was about to witness what many thought was "T.B.F.'s" madness. For hours the previous day negotiations between "T.B.F.", William Bolton, Hal McCabe and Frank Shaw continued in earnest all day at the office of Atkinson and Boyd, chartered accountants in Coleraine, finishing at the home of Major Jack Baxter. The following day Betty was at the office of Wray & Baxter where she was to see her boss putting his name to the document which committed him to the Bolton take-over. After a quick snack at Corr's Corner, "T.B.F.", Bertie Gillanders and their advisers went to the Headquarters of the Northern Bank to finalise the deal. What he didn't know was that the bank chief had sent down an order to the Manager at the Kilrea Branch, Tom McComb, saying, "Don't ask Mr. Thompson for any security." When "T.B.F." discovered this, he got the biggest lift of his business life, so far.

He then sold Craigmore Quarries to "Moore Bros.," Contractor of Ballyclare. He also sold the massive crusher. Following his policy of good managment, he called in Tommy Leighton, who previously worked for R. J. Maxwell & Sons Ltd., and had been Inspector of Quarries with the Ministry of Commerce, and he accepted the appointment as General Manager.

Tommy Leighton got the company up and running again successfully. Jimmy Telford continued to work for the company and brought in extra staff. June had seen the acquisition of Maxwell's and August the acquisition of Bolton's. A telex communication system had also been introduced to "T.B.F.'s"

Garvagh headquarters. Customers were to be facilitated when their orders for new machines could be traced immediately between factory and the distributor. A Pye radio telecommunication installation had also been introduced enabling "T.B.F.'s" headquarters to contact any of their mobiles as they operated throughout Northern Ireland and County Donegal. He was also at this time appointed sole distributor for the complete range of Komatsu Forklift Trucks in Northern Ireland and Eire. His whole sales and service organisation was now giving great attention to the reliability of their products. They emphasised constant data feed-back. They concentrated on ceaseless analysis. They carried out exhaustive studies and applied rigorous test procedures. They insisted on meticulous quality control. In truth it had been a long way from Nutt's to Bolton's, with J.C.B. and Komatsu thrown in!

"T.B.F." went, with Kathleen, at this time to Japan on a business trip for Komatsu Forklift trucks. "T.B.F." was the only man on the trip to take his wife with him and Kathleen thoroughly enjoyed the visit which took them, via Anchorage in Alaska to Tokyo, and then on to Osaka.

Sadly the news reached them in Japan of the sudden death of "T.B.F.'s" brother Billy at the early age of 62. It was a very sad home coming indeed.

In May, 1973, Kenneth H. Cheevers joined the T.B.F. Thompson (Garvagh) Group of Companies, and he with R. J. Gillanders, was to become a very important part of the triangle of management and eventually boardroom directorship that emerged between the three of them. Within 20 years these three were to become an extremely formidable team.

The book of Proverbs speaks of it being good "that a man bear the yoke in his youth" and Ken had, in his youth, a fairly heavy yoke to carry. He was in his third year at Queen's University reading for a degree in Civil Engineering when his father died and he had to return home to Cookstown and run the family butchery business. He returned to University, after one year, and finished his degree. He was soon able to leave the family business and join the Londonderry County Council as a Civil Engineer. He rose through the ranks gaining much valuable experience but felt, after sixteen years, that he had reached the situation where he needed to move on. Then the "Bee Charmer" called!

Ken recalls his first meeting with "T.B.F." at "Heathlands"; the memorable and meticulously tailored suit, the clean-shaven face, the ceaseless using of hands for expression, the sheer business drive of the man. Ken was very impressed but did something which he looks back on now as sheer youthful bravado; he dug his heels in and said he would accept the position of Contracts Manager on two important conditions; he must have a share of the profits and a right to buy shares in the company. He tells, with deep gratitude, of "T.B.F.'s" reaction.

The "Bee Charmer" could have shown him the door for his sheer audacity to enter the beehive, but he didn't! He gave him the position along with a company car and told him that if he proved himself after one year, he would grant him his request.

Ken "burnt rubber" that year in sheer terms of hard work and got his "spurs" at the end of it. He says he has always found an excitement in working with "T.B.F." Of all the things "T.B.F." has taught him, the thing that has impressed him most is "T.B.F.'s" absolute determination to make money honestly. He says that he has found, through "T.B.F.", that anyone in business who is constantly evasive and enigmatic will not succeed. As he puts it, "Money got dishonestly doesn't stick". If Ken got his way the title of this biography of T.B.F. Thompson would not just read "One move ahead", it would read, "At least one move ahead"!

Ken was soon to experience his boss take over one of Northern Ireland's biggest companies; the drama of it was to be like, he says, "the canary taking the cat"! First, though, before we tell that story, we must digress a little.

The "formidable team": K. H. Cheevers, R. J. Gillanders and Dr. T. B. F. Thompson

The Reverend W. P. Nicholson whose ministry had a profound spiritual effect on the life of "T.B.F."

The Rt. Hon. W. J. Morgan, Minister of Health and Social Services arrives with Mrs. W. P. Nicholson for the opening ceremony of the new Mission Hall in Garvagh, 11th November, 1967.

Crowds wait for the opening of the new Mission Hall at Garvagh.

Things go better after a cup of tea! People chat over refreshments after the opening of the new Mission Hall.

Section of the crowd at the Garvagh Crusade, July 1969.
Mr. Sam Kirk at the organ.

*The Evangelist,
Mr. Hedley G. Murphy,
with Dr. Paul Freed of
Trans World Radio,
Monte Carlo, at the
Garvagh Crusade.*

The "car park" at the Garvagh Crusade.

"T.B.F." at the King's Inn Golf Club, Freeport, Bahamas, with Kathleen, November 1969.

Billy Thompson, Kathleen and "T.B.F." at Billy's son Kenneth's wedding in August 1973

CHAPTER ELEVEN

"That man Nicholson, again"

CHILDREN LIKE TO BE CRADLED WHERE THEY ARE born, and, this applies in the spiritual life as well as the physical. Converted to Christ under the influence of Edna Burns, who, of course, took him to hear Rev. W. P. Nicholson on the night of his conversion, "T.B.F." was spiritually cradled under the ministry of this extraordinary Christian minister. To understand "T.B.F." it is necessary to understand Nicholson and his message.

It is not easy for people in a later generation to understand how very influential Nicholson was in his impact on the religious life of Northern Ireland in his day. He was born into a family of seven children on 3rd April, 1876 in Cottown near Bangor, County Down. His father was a captain in the Merchant Navy and young Nicholson went to sea at sixteen. He sailed around the world and loved life, particularly, "aloft". For some time he worked in railroad construction in South Africa.

His own conversion to Christ is worth repeating. After returning home from a spell abroad, he was sitting at his mother's fireside one morning in May, 1899, waiting for his breakfast. Suddenly he came under a deep conviction of having broken God's laws and of his spiritually prodigal condition.

He felt a deep urge to trust Christ as Saviour and did so on the spot. He described the experience in the following words; "Suddenly and powerfully and consciously, I was saved. Such a peace and freedom from fear, such a sweet assurance filled my soul. I turned to my mother and said, 'Mother, I am saved'. She looked at me and nearly collapsed, and said, 'When?' I said, 'Just now'. 'Where?' 'Here, where I am sitting'. She cried with joy unspeakable". In later years he used to say, "I have never had any doubts about my salvation. I never doubted my dear mother's word about my natural birth, and do you think it strange of me to take God's Word without a doubt or fear? I became a new creature and began hating sin."

Yielding his life completely to God, few evangelists were to lead such a sanctified, earnest Christian life. He entered the Bible Training Institute in Glasgow in 1901, founded under the influence of the great American evangelist Dwight L. Moody. Soon he was touring the world as a preacher, even helping in the great Chapman-Alexander Australian evangelistic missions of 1910. He pastored the St. George's Cross Tabernacle (now known as the Findlay Memorial Church) in Glasgow for a time and also engaged in evangelistic work in North America where he was ordained by the Carlisle, Pennsylvania, Presbytery of the Presbyterian Church in the United States on April 15, 1914.

In 1920 Nicholson returned to Northern Ireland for what he thought would be a short visit. He was to conduct missions in commemoration of Sir Joseph Maclay's two sons who had been killed in the great war. The power of the Holy Spirit in those services was something to be long remembered. In Portadown, Lurgan, Newtownards, Lisburn, Ballymena, and Belfast it was soon obvious that Nicholson was God's man for the hour. Hundreds upon hundreds were converted to Christ. In market and shop, in townhouse and slum, in street and tram, Nicholson's missions were the talk of the land.

"I wouldn't go to your mission", one proprietor told Nicholson, "Those folk are a lot of hypocrites. They won't pay their bills." "Can I borrow your account book?" said Nicholson. That night the evangelist mounted the mission platform. "I have here the account of a shop in town", he said, naming it, "It contains the names of folk who haven't paid their bills. If they are not paid quickly then I'll read their names out on a subsequent evening". DID that proprietor get his bills paid, quickly!?

The committee of Nicholson's Shankill Road Mission reported to the Presbyterian General Assembly in 1922 that at least 2,500 people had been converted to the Saviour during his meetings. The whole community was touched. Deputations of cabsmen, tramwaymen, gangs that lounged at street corners, groups of girls out of warehouses, smart young business men and women, people of leisure and wealth, students at university, employers and employees, all rising in testimony meetings and witnessing for the Master. Midweek prayer meetings formerly with ten or twenty in them were overflowing with hundreds of people. As the Methodist Weekly "Irish Christian Advocate" said, "We have had an appalling year in some respects but spiritually it has been glorious. The winds of God have been blowing over us and not for many years has our church had so fruitful a season."

Nicholson's mission in Londonderry in April 1922 saw 1,300 people pass through the enquiry rooms, set up for those seeking Christ after each service. On its final Sunday of the evangelistic mission over 200 people made a definite decision for Christ. January 1923 saw Nicholson back missioning in Belfast, this time in the east of the city with twenty churches co-operating. The Rev. W. Presley McVitie reported in March, 1923, that "Since the beginning of 1923 we have seen over 5,000 old men, young men and women and those of tender years deeply feeling their need of salvation; bowing in penitence at the feet of the Great Christ and professing to take Him as their Saviour, Lord and King".

"The labours of Rev. W. P. Nicholson were greatly owned of God especially among the humbler people and to a large extent those not connected with any church".

At Ravenhill Presbyterian Church a special "mens only" meeting was held. An amazing sight ensued. Hundreds of workmen from "The Island" marched to the church straight from the great shipyard where, of course, the "TITANIC" had been built. So great was the crush at the entrance to the church the pillar supporting the gates moved off its foundation. We are told that a special shed had to be opened in the shipyard to receive stolen goods from men who had been converted to Christ at Nicholson's meetings. Nicholson certainly had a rare sense of humour. No man is without faults and Nicholson had his critics but as Dr. Graham Scroggie said, "They may say what they like about Nicholson but after all the test of a man's work and words is the goods he delivers - and he has delivered the goods."

The lives that were influenced for Christ under Nicholson's powerful preaching certainly show, right up to this present generation, that he, under God, delivered the goods. The Christian Union at Queen's University has roots in the spiritual blessing surrounding the days of Nicholson. Whole generations of children in churches across the world have received Dr. Paul

White's famous "Jungle Doctor" stories for Sunday School prizes. Few of them would realise that Paul White, whose work for Christ in East Africa was so blessed of God was first converted to Christ in a little Mission Tent by a railway track in New Zealand listening to the preaching of W. P. Nicholson.

One hundred men were converted to Christ through him at Holy Trinity, Cambridge, during his mission there for the Cambridge Inter-Collegiate Christian Union. Quite a large percentage of those who came to Christ went into the Christian ministry, full time. On and on the influence of this one life dedicated to God has reverberated and no life was more deeply influenced by him than the life of T. B. F. Thompson.

It was during Nicholson's time that the Irish Alliance of Christian Workers' Unions was formed. These unions were non-denominational but were committed to prevailing prayer, holiness of living and the study of the Scriptures and their main emphasis was outreach in the preaching of the Gospel. "T.B.F." was made President of Garvagh Christian Workers' Union in November 1948, one year after his conversion and remained President until March 1994.

Through the years he kept in touch with Nicholson and it was under "T.B.F.'s" auspices that the great evangelist held his last services in Ireland. In 1958 he stayed three times with the Thompsons at "Heathlands" and as an 82 year old preached to an overflowing Presbyterian Hall on 24th May 1958 in Garvagh. "T.B.F." and his friends wanted to build Mr. & Mrs. Nicholson a bungalow where they could retire but they returned to the United States.

One year later, in the autumn of 1959, they left America on board the liner "THE MAURETANIA" intending to settle in Bangor. On the voyage the evangelist took seriously ill with a heart attack and was brought ashore at Cork where he was taken to the Victoria Hospital. He lay critically ill for two weeks and entered Christ's immediate presence on Thursday, 29th October, at the age of 83. He was buried in Clandeboye Cemetery and his grave is marked with a very appropriate Bible verse:

"John did no miracles; but all things that John spake of this Man (Jesus) were true and many believed on Him there". (John 10: 41-42).

In 1967 "T.B.F." built a modern mission hall in Garvagh and on Saturday, 11th November 1967, the Rev. W. P. Nicholson's widow performed the opening ceremony. For the most part of 45 years, apart from his attendance and involvement at his local Presbyterian Church, where he is now an elder, "T.B.F." has been present virtually every Sunday evening at the 8.15 evangelistic service in the Mission Hall at Garvagh.

All through the years of his Presidency of the Christian Workers' Union at Garvagh, "T.B.F." has encouraged the holding of evangelistic missions led by outstanding men of God. Much blessing followed the opening of the Mission Hall through the preaching of evangelists Messers Boland and Grant at the Garvagh C.W.U. "T. B. F.'s" niece, Valerie, was the first convert in the Mission Hall and is now principal of a Christian school in Australia. Her brother Kenneth continues to be associated with the Mission Hall as a committee member, and is very faithful in presiding at the organ from week to week.

Other evangelists have included Dr. W. M. Craig, Dr. John Girvan, Major Alistair Smith, Mr. and Mrs. Bert Wheeler, Rev. Sam Workman, and Faith Mission Pilgrims amongst many others. Another great friend of "T.B.F.'s" was Dr. John Wesley White who went on to become an Associate Evangelist with Dr. Billy Graham.

August 1969 saw an outstanding evangelistic effort in Garvagh. T.B.F. Thompson invited an organisation called Evangelical Outreach to erect a huge tent on his ground in Garvagh and to conduct an evangelistic mission under the preaching of the evangelist Hedley G. Murphy. The guest soloist throughout the services was Mrs. Pat Mills of East Kilbride in Scotland. The evangelist's brother, James D. Murphy conducted the massed choir and 30,000 people poured into Garvagh during the period of the services. There were many conversions, and, at the final service "T.B.F." told the capacity crowd, "Our hearts have been stirred and our souls blessed as we have listened to Mr. Murphy's clear presentation of the Gospel message. Above all we thank and praise God for the large number of souls who made a personal commitment to Christ during the crusade. I know that I am expressing the feeling of thousands in North West Ulster when I say, 'Thank God for the day this crusade came to Garvagh.'"

So it is that "T.B.F.", cradled, spiritually, in Nicholson's evangelistic missions, has been marked all his life by a deep enthusiasm for this form of evangelistic outreach. To this very day there is nothing gives him greater pleasure than getting behind a well organised, Christ-exalting series of evangelistic meetings. Many have lived to thank God for his enthusiasm.

"T.B.F." at his own desk at his Garvagh Headquarters.

♦ CHAPTER TWELVE ♦

"John Barleycorn gets the heave"

YOU WOULD NOT BE WITH "T.B.F." VERY LONG before you discovered that he is a very vigorous tee-totaller. He makes no bones about it: John Barleycorn is not welcome at his table and he bars him from the tables of his companies.

Of course, people think such a policy is simply impossible to implement in business, but, then, they haven't worked for T.B.F. Thompson! Challenged by a sermon from Major Alistair Smith of the Salvation Army at an Easter Convention in 1962 as to the necessity of a consistent walk with God, "T.B.F.'s" conscience became deeply disturbed by a fear of leading others into alcohol abuse by buying them alcoholic drinks in the course of business. Having been a heavy drinker himself he was well aware of the power of alcohol to wreck a person's life. He decided on the spot to never buy anyone an alcoholic drink again. He also decided that no employee of his would ever be given expenses for alcoholic drink, and, at the height of his business life, this included at least 2,200 employees. On the very week of the sermon he went to Dick Robinson, the

Managing Director of his new Belfast company on the Ravenhill Road and introduced the policy.

That Christmas and on every subsequent Christmas no company under "T.B.F.'s" direction has given alcohol as a Christmas gift; the sale of turkeys, though, has not suffered as a result of his ban on alcohol!

"T.B.F." is well aware that the Bible's references which bear directly on drinking appear to be ambivalent. For example, in Psalm 104: 14-15 the Psalmist says, "You make grass grow for the cattle and plants for man to use so that he can grow his crops and produce wine to make him happy, olive oil to make him cheerful, and bread to give him strength." On the other hand wine is rejected in Proverbs 23: 31-35 with the famous statement, "Don't let wine tempt you, even though it is rich red, even though it sparkles in the cup and it goes down smoothly. The next morning you will feel as if you have been bitten by a poisonous snake. Weird sights will appear before your eyes, and you will not be able to think or speak clearly. You will feel as if you were out on the ocean, seasick, swinging high up on the rigging of a tossing ship. 'I must have been hit', you will say; 'I must have been beaten up, but I don't remember it. Why can't I wake up? I need another drink.'"

In the New Testament the situation is equally ambivalent for John the Baptist had a reputation for being a total abstainer and our Lord did take wine. Limited drinking is implied as being acceptable in 1 Timothy 3: 8; Titus 2: 3; 1 Timothy 5: 23, while drunkenness is expressly condemned in Romans 13: 13, Galatians 5: 21 and Ephesians 5: 18.

"T.B.F." has always maintained that his stance on alcohol stems from the teaching of the Scriptures regarding the position of leaders. The Scriptures teach particularly that leaders are to recognise that others around them are "weak". This means there are those, even in the Christian community who have limited root to their faith, who have not yet developed strong, consistent habits of Christian living, whose consciences are still untrained and whose Christian lives are shallow and potentially at risk, especially in a crisis, or those whose walk with God is still not a close one. "T.B.F." believes that the test of a true leader is in his or her attitude and behaviour towards the weak and vulnerable. For, says Scripture, "We who are strong ought to bear with the failings of the weak, and not to please ourselves. Even Christ did not please Himself."

While it may be argued that the Scriptures allow a Christian to drink alcohol moderately, "T.B.F." feels that the over-riding principle is, as one Bible translation of 1 Corinthians 6: 12 has it, "Everything is permissible - but not beneficial; I will not be mastered by anything" and again in Romans 14: 16, "Do not allow what you consider good to be spoken of as evil". Whatever view other Christians may have on the subject, "T.B.F." has always been determined never to stumble the weak in this area and has believed since that night in Bangor in 1962 that "example power" is greater than people realise. He retorts to Christian social drinkers that if the only time they are seen to drink is at social functions, then their "example power" is actually at its highest there.

The effect of alcohol on the body is always depressant and inhibitory, i.e. negative. Paradoxically the effect of small doses appears to bring relaxation, to reduce a sense of stress, to give feelings of pleasure or well-being, but alcohol does that by actually depressing the normal inhibitory systems in the higher centres of the brain. For example, pre-prandial "drinks" at a lunch or party are supposed to lower people's inhibitions and allow them to mix more freely, to give them a feeling of excitement or pleasure and to reduce the normal stresses of meeting strangers.

The plain fact is that these drinks do this by "cheating" and exerting a depressant action on protective natural inhibitions rather than giving an added excitatory action. In any event this effect is short lived and often it takes more and more to produce the same effect, as many tens of thousands of people can testify regarding the dangers, for example, of "nightcap" drinking. Even in small doses alcohol produces a loss of efficiency, reduces one's critical abilities, slows one's reflexes and allows one's more basic instincts to emerge.

It is a fact that alcohol disease is the third public health problem after cancer and cardiovascular disease. The mortality of dependent and problem drinkers is three to four times that of the general population and life expectancy is reduced by about fifteen years. "T.B.F." very well knew 70% of problem drinkers are at work. Each year between eight and fourteen million working days are lost through alcohol abuse and eight hundred million pounds are lost to industry through absence due to alcohol.

In about 80% of all serious road accidents, alcohol is implicated because it causes dis-inhibition, impairs judgment and the processes of thinking and leads to impulsiveness. The sad fact is that in 90% of suicide attempts, alcohol is involved. It causes depression to worsen, leads to impaired thinking processes, and produces impetuous actions. In one year there are one hundred thousand arrests for drunkenness of which one thousand go to prison. Public drunkenness takes up eighty thousand hours of police time and the costs to the criminal justice system are between six and seven million pounds.

These facts and figures do not reflect the personal and persistent anguish, shame, emotional pain and private grief of husbands, wives, children and parents within the number of households represented by approximately 15% - 20% of the population. It is a rather frightening fact that children of alcoholics are people who have been robbed of their childhood.

In the book *Adult Children of Alcoholics*, Janet Woititz says that she has seen five year olds running entire families. Millions of children have seen at least one parent in the throws of the affliction and the effect upon them is catastrophic. It is a very sobering truth that adult children of alcoholics, according to research, have difficulty following a project from beginning to end.

They lie when it would be just as easy to tell the truth. They judge themselves without mercy. They have difficulty having fun. They take themselves very seriously. They have difficulty with intimate relationships and overreact to changes to which they have no control. They constantly seek approval and affirmation and feel that they are different from other people. They are super responsible or super irresponsible. They are extremely loyal, even in the face of evidence that the loyalty is undeserved and tend to lock themselves into a course of action without giving consideration to the consequences.

"T.B.F." believes that if he is encouraging people to drink less at his end of the spectrum, then it is going to percolate down to the other end where the heavy drinkers are. Instead of being vilified by his business colleagues across Europe, he has constantly been admired for his stance. The picture contemporary society is throwing up is that the amount of alcohol that is consumed in this country is directly related to the number of social problems we have. It is easy therefore to respect deeply a person like T.B.F. Thompson who, in the light of this picture, remains a tee-totaller. He has wisdom on his side, however else he may be regarded.

"T.B.F.'s" policy on alcohol was never tested more directly than when he took over the Northern Ireland construction giant, Farrans. Farrans was formed in 1941 and there were few branches of building and civil engineering contracting in which it had not been successfully engaged. Its projects had included motorways and bridges, airfields, dock and harbour works, power stations, reservoirs and flats, telephone exchanges, colleges and university buildings, factories, supermarkets and shopping centres, offices, public authority houses and privately owned developments. Its activities had extended to the Near and Middle East, where extensive road works, an airfield, power stations, marine and building works had been constructed.

Its list of distinguished clients in the United Kingdom had included the Air Ministry, the Ministry of Defence, the Ministry of Public Building and Works, the War Department, the Scottish Home Department, and the Northern Ireland Departments of Commerce, Environment, Finance, Health and Social Services, the Jordanian Ministry of Public Works and Transport and the United States of America Department of the Navy. Its work for County Councils had included Antrim, Armagh, Down, Donegal, Dumfriesshire, Hampshire, Lanarkshire, Peebleshire, Roxburghshire, Tyrone, Wigtownshire, the Grampian Regional Council and the Belfast District Council. Industrial and commerical clients stretched from British Oxygen to B.P., from Courtaulds to the Ford Motor Company, from Rolls Royce to United Molasses, from Grand Metropolitan Hotels to the Goodyear Tyre and Rubber Company.

In Northern Ireland Farrans' work touched every corner of the Province. They had built amongst other projects the Maydown Textile Factory in Londonderry, the Silverwood Estate in Craigavon, miles of the M2 motorway in County Antrim, the General Aircraft apron at Belfast International Airport, the Antrim Forum Recreation Centre, and the most bombed hotel in Western Europe, the famous Europa in Belfast.

When it came to the ear of "T.B.F." that Farrans might be sympathetic to a take-over bid, he knew that if he was to respond and win the company to his Group, he would be facing, by far, the biggest challenge in all of his business career. He gathered his advisers around him and asked the question he always asked at such junctures: "What is the worst that can happen if we buy Farrans and we have, say, a big job in England or Wales not yet finished? Can we lose £250,000 if our judgment isn't good? Can we lose £500,000 or £750,000 or £1,000,000 maximum?". The answer his advisers gave him was that he could not lose as the company was in profit. "O.K.!" replied the Bee Charmer, "If we don't lose more than a million we will have a go, provided that Mr. Sam Taggart, the Managing Director and I can agree a price."

Sam Taggart began negotiations with "T.B.F." backed up by his team and particularly John Brown, his expert on the commercial aspect of Farrans. Mr. Taggart, in the midst of these negotiations, was in for a big surprise. "If I take over this company there will be no alcohol of any kind", said "T.B.F." He did not mean that he would stop his employees drinking alcohol but he did mean that they would get no expenses for it from the business and that at no function of the company would alcohol be given. "Tom, you couldn't run this business without it", said Sam Taggart. "There will be no deal, then," said Tom.

Whatever view people take of "T.B.F.'s" stance on drink, one thing is for certain, he is prepared to pay a dear price for his convictions on the subject. He was prepared to turn down the ownership of a company with an annual turnover of at least £50million if alcohol was a must in the running of the business.

The deal went through and "T.B.F." took over Farrans in 1977. At the first board meeting a statement from the minutes makes fascinating reading, "At the outset the Chairman declared that the policy of the company in the future regarding the purchase of wines and spirits would be the same as in the

Garvagh Group, viz. In no circumstances will the company incur expenditure on the purchase of alcoholic drinks nor will any employee be reimbursed through their entertaining expenses for the provision of same. Mr. Thompson said that Atkinson & Boyd the new Auditors for the company had strict instructions to disallow any expenditure of this kind found on invoices and intimated that the matter was not negotiable." The company had a very luxurious head office on Park Lane in London but "T.B.F." was still, even at the heady heights he had now reached, an Ulsterman, and, what is more, a Garvagh man. He could have become the big time tycoon in his lifestyle, moved to the London scene and dazzled people with his success. But he sold the Park Lane Office and was more than content to live on in Garvagh.

"T.B.F." offered Mr. Sam Taggart, the former Managing Director of Farrans, a seat on the Board of Farrans when he took it over. Though grateful for the kindness of "T.B.F." in offering, Mr. Taggart declined as he did not feel he wanted such responsibility at 72 years of age. "T.B.F." then insisted that Mr. Taggart be allowed to keep his personal driver, his personal secretary, his office and his Jaguar car. Seven months later at a Cement Society Dinner in London, Mr. Taggart was found dead in his chair. "T.B.F." was very glad that he had made no major changes in Mr. Taggart's life.

"How do you measure success?," wrote Ralph Waldo Emerson. "To laugh often and much; to win the respect of intelligent people and the affection of children; to earn the appreciation of honest critics and endure the betrayal of false friends; to appreciate beauty; to find the best in others; to leave the world a bit better, whether by ..... a redeemed social condition, or a job well done ...... this is to have succeeded".

It is fascinating that Emerson doesn't once mention fame, money, status, rank, power over others, position or a dazzling self-image. He doesn't even mention size or numbers or statistics.

"T.B.F." took his stance on alcohol, and successfully became Chairman and Managing Director and chief shareholder of one of the biggest companies in the history of the construction industry in Northern Ireland. He was one move ahead, for sure, but not by mere willpower or gift. "For promotion comes neither from the east nor from the west nor from the south", says the Scriptures, "But God is the Judge". "T.B.F." has never believed in a prosperity Gospel which teaches that if a person seeks first the kingdom of God they are automatically bound to prosper materially. "T.B.F." knew very well that more people have died for the cause of Christ in the twentieth century than in any other. He knew very well that for many following Christ has not meant material prosperity but the very opposite.

He knew in his heart that God had prospered him for a reason and entered the late 1970s with a deep conviction that, as the Scriptures put it, "to whom much is given is much expected". Alexander Solzhenitsyn once asked "Must one point out that from ancient times a decline in courage has been considered the beginning of the end?" "T.B.F." was going to need a lot of courage for what lay ahead if he was to steadily hold the very full cup which had been handed to him.

"T.B.F." and R. J. Gillanders at Balmoral Show in 1975 as they
"flood the country" with J.C.Bs.

"T.B.F." with Norman Emerson (fourth from left), the man who with
Sam Gilchrist bought two J.C.B. loading shovels at the London Plant
Show in the presence of J. C. Bamford without
knowing or naming a price!

♦ CHAPTER THIRTEEN ♦

"Shut the door, there's more!"

"**T**.B.F." HAD CERTAINLY MOVED ON SINCE THE day he bought Felix Doherty's small lorry for £70 and went up and down the countryside looking for business. At this stage in our journey through his life, a pause to list what he had achieved is an interesting exercise.

The T.B.F. Thompson (Garvagh) Group now comprised of the following. In building and civil engineering; Farrans Ltd., Farrans (Construction) Ltd., Farrans (London) Ltd. In quarrying, road construction and surfacing; R. J. Maxwell & Son Ltd., W.M. Bolton & Sons Ltd., R. J. Maxwell (Ballymena) Ltd., J. T. Glover Ltd., Ramsey Bros. (Asphalt) Ltd., North Down Quarries Ltd., John McLean & Sons (Quarries) Ltd. In plant and equipment distributors and mechanical handling; T. B. F. Thompson (Garvagh) Ltd., T. B. F. Thompson (Ireland) Ltd., Strangford Ltd., North Down Engineering Co. (Belfast) Ltd., Strangford (Plant) Ltd., T. B. F. Thompson (Engineering) Ltd., T. B. F. Thompson (Plant) Ltd, W. H. Beckett & Co. Ltd.

In material suppliers the Group owned Ready Use Concrete Co. Ltd., Scott (Toomebridge) Ltd., Lough Neagh Sand, Roofing, Tiles and Concrete Products, the Lough Neagh Sand Co. Ltd., Readyuse Scott Ltd., Carmean Lime Works Ltd., Agricultural and Industrial Limestone Products, Ready Use Scott Marketing Ltd., Irish Ready Use Ltd. In property development the Group owned Ardis Estates Ltd. and T. B. F. Thompson (Properties) Ltd. In finance, Garvagh Securities Ltd. and T.B.F. Thompson Finance Ltd.

In Northern Ireland when someone has to ask the way somewhere they should bear in mind that the populace have their own expressions for distance. For example, "'Sneer a mile" is an expression which signifies a distance of slightly less than one mile. "'Sa feer wee distance" signifies a distance of up to five miles. "Two shakes of a lamb's tail" is about five hundred yards and "hardly a beagle's gowl away" is about three-quarters of a mile. Probably the most amusing of all of these expressions is "ye cud be there before yer back!". This signifies a distance of about two to three hundred yards. "Ye cud be there before yer back" could also describe, aptly, the experience "T.B.F." had following his acquisition of Farrans.

Towards the end of 1978 the T. B. F. Thompson Group was approached by Cement-Roadstone with its headquarters at Belgard Castle in the Republic of Ireland. Cement-Roadstone owned 2 billion tons of strategically placed stone, sand and gravel reserves and operated in over seventy locations. It was the sole cement producer in the Republic of Ireland. Active also in the United Kingdom, the Netherlands, Cyprus and in the Mountain States of the U.S.A. Cement-Roadstone was interested in buying the T. B. F. Thompson Group.

The "Bee Charmer" decided that this nest was worth settling in. He began yet another round of negotiations and after two sets of accountants had worked for quite a long time he called a meeting for the merger at "Heathlands".

There were few nights more important in "T.B.F.'s" business career than the night of the Cement-Roadstone - T. B.F. Thompson (Group) Merger. Solicitors and accountants from Dublin and Belfast sat down to dinner at 6.30 p.m. at "Heathlands" and after a hearty meal with friendly banter they got down to work. Four rooms in "T.B.F.'s" home were occupied as the final details of the merger were drawn up and after a very exhausting evening "T.B.F." sold his group at 4.30 a.m.

It was, of course, a very wise move on "T.B.F.'s" part. He was aware of the complex inheritance tax implications if he should suddenly die and he knew that this left the T.B.F.-Farrans' staff with a certain feeling of vulnerability because their main concern was for their security and long term future. It was a case of what was good for "T.B.F." was good for all who were employed by his group and he knew it. The merger removed the feeling of vulnerability.

When Cement-Roadstone had first approached the merger they had applied to the Northern Bank to find out its opinion of T. B. F. Thompson. The reaction of the bank is worth quoting. Of the man who first deposited £25 in their bank agency at Garvagh so many years before, they now wrote, "We can't praise him too highly - entrepreneur, leading businessman, unblemished reputation, 'a man of his word', this bank would support him through thick and thin. We know that Cement-Roadstone and the T. B. F. Thompson (Garvagh) Group were having talks and if "T.B.F." does a deal he will honour his commitment to the letter. He will not stray off course ....." Cement-Roadstone knew their man.

As everyone at "Heathlands" started heading home at 4.30 a.m. "T.B.F." suddenly turned to his advisors Stanley Hill,

Senior Partner, Carson and McDowell, solicitors, Frank Shaw and Derek Irwin, Partners in the firm of Atkinson and Boyd, chartered accountants, as they started for the door and said, "Boys, we are not finished, yet". Fairly exhausted by this time, they wondered what on earth "T.B.F." could mean. "Kathleen and I", said "T.B.F.", "are going to form two Trusts this morning. We want to transfer valuable assets into them immediately." It was at that early hour of the morning that instructions were given to form the T. B. F. Thompson Trust and the Kathleen L. Thompson Trust for the benefit of philanthropic work based on Christian principles. Those who were involved in drawing up the Trusts were staggered at "T.B.F.'s" move and in a very real sense many people were soon to discover that "T.B.F." was to fulfil within the next few years the worth of John Bunyan's little couplet which said:

"There was a man, they called him mad,
The more he gave the more he had."

Bernard Baruch once said: "Whatever failures I have known, whatever errors I have committed, whatever follies I have witnessed in private and public life, have been the consequences of action without thought". "T.B.F." on the night he sold his group had his priorities right. It may have been 4.30 a.m. but he had a priority that he had long thought about fulfilling. His was no spontaneous, spur-of-the-moment action. He had long planned it in his heart.

Now was his moment. It was as the Apostle Paul put it to the Christians at Ephesus: "Look carefully, then, how you walk! Live purposefully and worthily and accurately, not as the unwise and witless, but as wise - sensible intelligent people: Making the very most of the time, buying up each opportunity because the days are evil. Therefore do not be vague and thoughtless and foolish, but understanding and firmly grasping what the will of the Lord is." (Ephesians 5:15-17 Amplified

Bible) "T.B.F." believed God's will for him was to set up the Trusts and carefully, before any other move, he set them in motion for the benefit of other people. It has proved to be one of the wisest moves he has ever made.

To "T.B.F.'s" great surprise he was offered a seat as a director on the Board of Cement-Roadstone. He took his seat on 18th July 1979 and held it until he retired from the position in 1985. Cement-Roadstone asked him to remain Chairman of T.B.F. Thompson (Garvagh) Ltd., which he did. That year Cement- Roadstone sales were IR £258 million and its profits were IR £24 million and the group employed 7,142 people on average. The shares of the company were quoted on the Dublin and London Stock Exchange and there were 14,500 shareholders.

The total assets of Cement-Roadstone were IR £265 million.

The board meetings were always held, once a month, at Pembroke Street in Dublin or at Belgard Castle. "T.B.F." travelled by train, car or plane (always insisting on two pilots in case one got into difficulties!) and loved the cut and thrust of this international and ever expanding company. The Chairman was Dr. Michael Dargan who was also Chairman of Aer Lingus, followed by Des Trainor on Dr. Dargan's retirement. The able Jimmy Culliton, a Chief Executive in "T.B.F.'s" time was followed by Tony Barry, men "T.B.F." respected very much.

Big decisions were made in these meetings and "T.B.F." became very much a part of the decision making process. One of Cement-Roadstone's directors would, in turn, travel once a month to Garvagh to board meetings of T.B.F. Thompson (Garvagh) Ltd. and sixteen people would regularly sit down at "Heathlands" for lunch. "T.B.F." showed that cross-border business in Ireland was totally acceptable in his books and to this day cannot speak highly enough of his colleagues in the

Republic of Ireland. He never had any problem with them and when pressed on his view of the future maintains that, despite terrorism, times are not hopelessly bad in Ireland, North and South, and he refuses to countenance phrases like "this country is finished". He looks on it as negative thinking and has constantly refused in his life to be a negative thinker.

"When you are a negative thinker you are finished", he constantly maintains. A new group was soon to emerge under his influence to prove that right up to the wire of the new century and all in the face of repeated onslaughts of terrorism, the expertise, initiative, skills and verve of business, even in Belfast, can rival any other place. "T.B.F.'s" view is not, as modern journalists would say, a "Hello" magazine attitude. It is totally realistic.

There is a trace of Norman Vincent Peale's "power of positive thinking" in "T.B.F.'s" approach to life. He freely admits to being influenced by Dr. Peale's books and has not been slow to give copies of his works to numerous people throughout his lifetime. Perhaps his favourite Peale quote is, "Try really try. Think really think. Believe really believe."

When "T.B.F." flew home to Aldergrove Airport from his very last Cement-Roadstone meeting in Cork and slipped into a function at Dunadry Inn that evening, it was not with thoughts of retirement on his mind. The world might have viewed Northern Ireland, with its civil and sectarian strife of the late 1970's and 80's as a poisoned community with no hope for the future but such was not the view of this "country boy from Garvagh". He was, as Northern Ireland people say, "rarin' to go", again.

He had his eye on what others called a "cash trap" company with which he had had long association in one way or another.

Now a public company "T.B.F." had his eye on Charles Hurst Ltd. He had been buying shares in the company for over ten years but one day the motor cycling C. T. Hurst, O.B.E. arrived at "Heathlands" and, out of the blue and under absolutely no pressure from "T.B.F." offered him half of his shares in Charles Hurst Ltd.! This gave "T.B.F." a 29.4% share of the company. He now either had to sit in that position or make a take-over bid. As the Manchester Evening Standard stated at the time, "Why has Ulster businessman Tom Thompson bought ... very expensively ... in the loss-making Charles Hurst, the Northern Ireland car dealers?" Northern Ireland was about to find out.

130

The Farrans takeover in 1977.
Standing (from left): R. J. Gillanders (TBFT), K. H. Cheevers (TBFT), P. Osmond (Farrans), J. Brown,
J. G. Berry, J. A. McCullough, D. I. McClure, D. L. R. Miles (Farrans)
Seated (from left): W. A. Toner, S. Taggart (Farrans), "T.B.F.", R. W. Watts (Farrans) and Kathleen Thompson.

"T.B.F." and Kathleen in Brussels after the official acceptance of the Industrial John Deere franchise in 1979.

A Cement-Roadstone Holdings/TBF Thompson (Garvagh) Group "get-together" at "Heathlands". From left (seated): J. P. Culliton (Chief Executive, CRH), "T.B.F.", Dr. M. Dargan (Chairman, CRH Holdings & Aer lingus) and J. B. Newland (Director, Northern Bank) From left (back row): T. McComb (Manager, Northern Bank, Kilrea), R. J Gillanders and K. H. Cheevers (TBFT), D. Bryant (Director, Northern Bank), D. Roche (Director, CRH), A. D. Barry (Director, CRH), W. Ervin (Director, Northern Bank).

"T.B.F." in South Africa in 1981.

CHAPTER FOURTEEN

"That's all I've got; there's nothing else!"

"**T**.B.F."AND HIS WIFE KATHLEEN HAD ALWAYS believed that God is a guide. They prayed to Him for guidance in the decisions they made and often experienced the awareness that God was actually going before them, opening up their way. "T.B.F." and Kathleen would have always believed that the Lord was the ultimate "Managing Director" of their businesses. Not everyone might appreciate such a description of God but perhaps a story might help.

A Pastor, dressed in a comfortable pair of old blue jeans, once boarded a plane to return home. He settled into the last unoccupied seat next to a well dressed businessman with the "Wall Street Journal" tucked under his arm. The Pastor, a little embarrassed over his casual attire, decided he would look straight ahead and, stay out of any in-depth conversation. But the plan didn't work. The man greeted him, so, to be polite, the Pastor asked about the man's work. Let the Pastor tell the story: "I'm in the figure salon business. We can change a woman's self-concept by changing her body. It's really a very profound, powerful thing," answered the businessman. His pride spoke between the lines.

"You look my age," I said. "Have you been at this long?"

"I just graduated from the University of Michigan's School of Business Administration. They have given me so much responsibility already, and I feel very honoured. In fact I hope to eventually manage the western part of the operation."

"So, you are a national organisation?" I asked, becoming impressed despite myself.

"Oh, yes. We are the fastest growing company of our kind in the nation. It's really good to be part of an organisation like that, don't you think?"

I nodded approvingly and thought, "Impressive. Proud of his work and accomplishments ... Why can't Christian's be proud like that? Why are we so often apologetic about our faith and our church?"

Looking askance at my clothing, he asked the inevitable question, "And what do you do?"

"It's interesting that we have similar business interests," I said. "You are in the body-changing business; I'm in the personality changing business. We apply basic theocratic principles to accomplish indigenous personality modification."

He was hooked, but I knew he would never admit it. (Pride is powerful)

"You know, I've heard about that," he replied hesitatingly. "But do you have an office here in the city?"

"Oh, we have many offices. We have offices up and down the state. In fact, we are national: we have at least one office in every state of the union including Alaska and Hawaii."

He had this puzzled look on his face. He was searching his mind to identify this huge company he must have read or heard about, perhaps in his "Wall Street Journal".

"As a matter of fact, we've gone international. And Management plan to put at least one office in every country of the world by the end of this business era."

I paused. "Do you have that in your business?" I asked.

"Well, no. Not yet," he answered. "But you mentioned management. How do they make it work?"

"It's a family concern. There's a Father and a Son ... and they run everything."

"It must take a lot of capital," he asked, sceptically.

"You mean money?" I asked. "Yes, I suppose so. No one knows just how much it takes, but we never worry because there's never a shortage ... in fact those of us in the Organisation have a saying about our Boss, 'He owns the cattle on a thousand hills.'"

"Oh, He's into ranching too?" asked my captive friend.

"No, its just a saying we have to indicate His wealth."

My friend sat back in his seat, musing over our conversation.

"How is it with you?" he asked.

"The employees? They are something to see," I said. "They have a 'Spirit' that pervades the organisation. It works like this; the Father and Son love each other so much that their love filters down through the organisation who are willing to die for me. Do you have that in your business?" I was almost shouting now. People were starting to shift noticeably in their seats.

"Not yet," he said. Quickly changing strategies, he asked, "But do you have good benefits?"

"They are substantial," I countered, with a gleam. "I have complete life insurance, fire insurance - all the basics. You might not believe that it's true; I have holdings in a mansion that's being built right now for my retirement. Do you have that in your business?"

"Not yet," he answered, wistfully. The light was dawning.

"You know, one thing bothers me about all you're saying. I've read the journals, and if your business is all you say it is, why haven't I heard about it before now?"

"That's a good question," I said. "After all, we have a 2000 year old tradition."

"Wait a minute!" he said.

"You're right," I interrupted. "I'm talking about the church."

"I knew it. You know, I'm Jewish."

"Want to sign up?" I asked.

Tom and Kathleen Thompson had signed up and served the Lord, the 'Managing Director' of their busy lives over a very long period, but, sadly, Kathleen's earthly service came to a very sudden end in July 1986. A Nursing Sister who gained her SRN at Londonderry City and County Hospital and her SCM at the Royal Victoria Hospital in Belfast, Kathleen had long been a committee member of the Garvagh-Kilrea Combat Cancer Group. The very thing she fought against appeared suddenly in her life. Treatment at first appeared to be successful and on Friday, July 4th, 1986 Tom went to the Coleraine Hospital expecting to be taking Kathleen home very soon. He was to find that suddenly she had indeed "gone Home to be with Christ, which is far better." He could hardly believe it. They had enjoyed 38 years of happily married life together.

The surgeon, Mr. John Matthews, took Tom aside and broke the news, gently. He had realised Kathleen's life was slipping away and had said to her comfortingly, "God loves you, Christ died for you." Kathleen looked up at him and with deep assurance said, "That's all I've got - there is nothing else!" and died.

"Today," said Dr. John Girvan in the course of his funeral address, "Mrs. Thompson is gazing in the face of Him she had learned to love and serve. She has come to know in a very real way the truth of the words quoted by Paul in 1 Corinthians 2 verse 9 - "Eye hath not seen nor ear heard, neither has it entered into the heart of man, the things which God has prepared for them that love Him."

He then asked his congregation to ask themselves three vital questions: "How long have I to live? What am I living for? What will become of me when I die?" He then gave the Bible's answer to these stirring questions.

"While," continued Dr. Girvan, "In this world of God's making there were things she valued, she nevertheless made preparation to live in that City that hath foundations whose builder and maker is God."

Mrs. Kathleen Thompson was buried in the family burying ground at St. Paul's Parish Church, Garvagh and today her memory is perpetuated by the T. B. F. Thompson Ministries Headquarters in Garvagh. The building was dedicated at a special service on November 1st, 1986.

At this dedication ceremony a very special tape was released incorporating Kathleen's favourite hymns, sung by Mildred Rainey. Mrs. Rainey also composed a very beautiful song based on Kathleen's last words, entitled "God Loves Me" which is also included in the tape. To date in excess of 60,000 copies of this tape have been distributed.

The Fold Housing Association for the elderly asked that their local development be named after Kathleen. The "Kathleen L. Thompson Fold" stands in Garvagh today as a very fitting memorial to a very caring lady.

Kathleen had remained anchored to one great truth - God loved her and Christ had died for her and for Kathleen there was, ultimately, nothing else. Ultimately, there isn't. The Pastor on the aircraft was right; the Lord's business will outlast all others.

The main Charles Hurst Group complex on 15 acres at Boucher Road, Belfast, comprising materials and services ranging from multi-franchise vehicles, (including leasing and contract hire), to fuels, tyres and insurances.

Another Charles Hurst development at Newtownabbey opened October 1995.

♦ CHAPTER FIFTEEN ♦

"The milk in the coconut"

TALK TO ANYONE WHO HAS HAD CLOSE DEALINGS with "T.B.F." and they will tell you that he has incredible powers of concentration. Maybe this strength has, at times, proved to be a fault for when he is on to something he blocks everything else out to concentrate on the project in hand and others, who have important decisions to make in middle management cannot immediately get to him. Those powers of concentration, though, have saved companies, rescued jobs, made him, constantly, in his business life, one move ahead.

It is important to "T.B.F." to concentrate on projects that are worthwhile and vital and not to focus on merely good projects while missing the best. It's a bit like the lady who was lonely and thought she had better do something about it, as the loneliness was killing her.

She decided to get a pet and dropped into a nice pet store one afternoon to look over the selection. The pet store owner proved most helpful and advised her that he thought one of his prize parrots would be the answer to her problem.

He assured her it was a real chatter-box with a friendly disposition and a wide vocabulary. Yes, it was very expensive, but it would prove to be almost like another human being in the house.

The lady was delighted and bought the expensive parrot along with a large and very elegant cage. But a problem soon emerged. The bird never said a word in a full week! She thought she had better investigate and stopped by the pet shop.

"And how's the parrot doing?" said the pet shop owner. "I'm sure he never shuts up!"

"I haven't been able to get a single word out of that bird all week", said the frustrated lady, "I'm really worried about it".

"Madam", said the pet shop owner, "Did you buy a mirror when you got the parrot and the cage last week?".

"A mirror? No."

"Oh, I assure you that a parrot needs a mirror", said the pet shop owner.

"The strange thing about parrots is that after they see themselves they begin to feel comfortable, and, in no time at all, I'm sure this one will begin to talk."

So the lady bought a mirror and put it into the cage. Try as she might the lady simply could not get the bird to talk. For hours she would keep chatting to the parrot but it just stared at her in silence. Another full week passed without a word and by now the lady was getting really up-tight about the whole thing.

"That parrot you sold me simply isn't talking." she told the pet store owner.

"Did you buy a ladder when you got the cage?" said the pet shop owner.

"A ladder? No. I didn't know a parrot needed a ladder. Will that make it talk?"

"Of course it will. The parrot will look in the mirror and after a bit of exercise climbing up and down the ladder it will be talking in no time. You simply won't believe what you will hear. You really do need a ladder."

The lady bought the ladder, put it into the cage next to the mirror and waited and after two weeks there was still not a single sound. By now she was reaching panic stage.

"Why doesn't it talk?", she said as she returned to the store in tears with the same complaint.

"Madam, I'm sorry but I forgot to tell you that parrots need a swing", said the pet store owner.

"A swing? I have a cage and a mirror and a ladder and I thought I had everything. What would I need a swing for?".

"You just simply have to have a swing. With a swing a parrot feels completely at home. It glances in the mirror, strolls up and down the ladder, and before long it's on the swing. A swinging parrot really talks!"

The woman bought the swing and attached it to the top of the cage near the ladder and coaxed the parrot up the ladder and on to the swing.

For another twelve days not a single sound came from the cage. Suddenly, she came bursting into the pet store at "high doh."

The owner came forward eagerly and said, "How's the parrot? I'm sure" - " The parrot is dead at the bottom of the cage!"said the irate lady.

"Well that is absolutely terrible" said the store owner, "I am just terribly shocked about it all.Did it, Madam, just happen to say anything at all before it died?"

"Yes, as a matter of fact, it did," said the lady

"As it lay there taking in its last few breaths it said, very faintly, 'Don't they have any FOOD down at that store?'"

Essentials are important to "T.B.F." and he concentrates on them. Yes, he once owned a Rolls Royce and even got caught speeding in it with a Presbyterian Moderator on board! Yes, he did once arrive in his Rolls Royce when the Presbyterian General Assembly was meeting in Dublin and the local police force and dignitaries thought it was the Irish President arriving and snapped immediately to attention! Yes, he has flown to Washington and dined at Presidential Prayer Breakfasts. Yes, he enjoys holidays abroad. Yes, he has hosted a luncheon for community and religious leaders and members at the House of Lords. These, of course, are only a few of his extra curricular activities but they are not the essentials in his life. He has not spent his days pining for the trappings of business, it is the business itself that gives him buzz, adrenalin and immense self-fulfilment.

"T.B.F.'s" adrenalin was flowing at Christmas 1984. He and his fellow directors, R. J. Gillanders and K. H. Cheevers (T.B.F. Thompson Ltd.) had just employed the merchant bankers Warburg to help prepare a take-over bid for Charles Hurst Ltd. The shares were 50p in the Financial Times and after much deliberation a letter was sent to Mr. Toby Hurst by hand, offering, on a buy or sell basis, to purchase his shares at well above the market price.

After the war, of course, there had been a post-war boom and Hurst's had emerged to obtain franchises for Rover, MG, Renault and Jaguar-Daimler cars. By 1972 it had become a public company. It was a coconut worth cracking.

"T.B.F." of course had had his eye on the Hurst coconut for a long time and on 22nd May 1985 T.B.F. Thompson Ltd. became the new owners of Charles Hurst Ltd. The coconut had been broken and milk began to flow in an amazing fashion. The company had been strung out over different centres on Adelaide Street, Antrim Road, Boucher Road and Saintfield Road in Belfast, and also at Dundonald and Portadown. The new management decided to move the main franchises to the fourteen and a half acre site at Boucher Road and a whole new concept for car sales emerged.

There are, today, few complexes throughout Europe that even come close to the multi-franchise choice of new or used cars offered at the Hurst Auto-complex.

No wonder the company receives at least 100,000 telephone calls a month!

If you were to take a walk around the huge site, one of the largest of its kind in Western Europe, with its showrooms and workshops, you would find that it resembles a miniature motor show. You could visit one of the largest Nissan dealerships in the United Kingdom based at the Nissan showroom at Boucher Road. You could view the Renault car showroom or visit the Landrover Centre. This complex also contains the Ferrari franchise for all of Ireland and the Citroen franchise for all of Belfast. There is, of course, the Damlier-Jaguar showroom but if the large "cats" are not to your taste, you could always visit the Hurst motor cycle centre who are the distributors of BMW, Yamaha, Kawasaki, Triumph, Ducati and Honda Motor cycles. You could also be taught how to ride a motor cycle and you would be able to buy all the gear you need to face all kinds of weather and conditions. There are eight thousand square feet of showroom on which you and your friends could talk "bikes"!

Of course if you want a Bentley that's available too but if the Bentley is too slow for you, you could always buy the world's fastest and most expensive production car ever made, the

Jaguar XJ220. This 220 m.p.h. supercar has a mighty 542 B.H.P. V6 turbo-charged engine. In the midst of all of your walk around this amazing complex, you could take a break at the restaurant and mull over a coffee. If you needed a new tyre you could go to one of the five bays at the Boucher Road site and have it fitted to your car. You would see tyres coming in on containers direct from the manufacturers from various countries such as South Korea, Holland and Belgium. All tyre requirements for car, truck, tractor, or motor cycles are available in an ever changing market. If you had a damaged car you could of course get it repaired at the Charles Hurst Body Shop and if you wanted to lease a car you could do so from a purpose built premise on the Hurst Auto Complex from where the current fleet of 2,000 contract cars are controlled. Any make of new vehicle can be supplied. There is also a vast growth in the parts business at the Boucher Road Complex. Known as Unipart, it boasts of "thousands of parts for millions of vehicles". The boast is not an idle one because at Boucher Road there are 500,000 stocks covering in some degree over 90% of cars on the road. Apart of course from the highly successful finance side of Charles Hurst's known as Adelaide Finance, there is also the ever expanding Adelaide Insurance Services.

As insurance premiums have increased dramatically over the past few years, Charles Hurst customers have been increasingly seeking advice from the sales personnel at Boucher Road as to where and from whom to purchase. As a result of this obvious need, Adelaide Insurance Services was established to provide expert and professional advice on all general insurance matters. Success to date of this side of the company has been remarkable.

Within the financial services sector of Charles Hurst a new Pensions and Financial Services company has also recently been formed.

There is one remarkable statistic in all of this growth. The turnover of Charles Hurst Ltd. by 1985 was £65 million. The turnover at 1994 was £158 million, and for 1995 almost £200 million.

The motto of the company is "Still Growing and Still Caring" and that remains true to this day. Although you could buy a Rolls Royce, an Aston Martin or a Ferrari at Boucher Road, you could also buy a Mini as well. Plans are afoot to develop, at Quarry Corner, near Newtownards, another "mini" Boucher Road complex on a three acre site. The new Newtownabbey complex covers North Belfast and the County Antrim area.

Hurst's, of course, have long been involved as a distributor of a variety of oils in Northern Ireland and had sister companies supply products in parts of Scotland and the North of England. The company was originally involved with Shell-Max and BP. Then the brand separation came in 1973 when BP Marketing was established. BP oil itself came into being in 1976 and, a year later, the distribution network expanded with the formation of Hurst Fuels Ltd. with its headquarters at Kilmarnock and depots at Dumfries, Stranraer and Dalston in the North of England. Completing the picture was Arran Oils Ltd. which distributed all BP oil products from its depot at Brodick on the Isle of Arran.

In 1988 re-structuring within the B.P. Oil network resulted in Hurst Fuels Ltd. being appointed sole distributors for B.P. Oil U.K. Ltd. throughout the whole of Northern Ireland.

Deeply involved in the expansion of Hurst Fuels was Mr. Fred Maguire who lived for quite some time at Troon in Ayrshire heading up operations and who is now Chief Executive Charles Hurst Ltd. Fred smiles when he recalls that "T.B.F." first started in the oil business when he innovated the paraffin drum under the driver's seat in his grocery lorry working up Glenullin in 1934! The Charles Hurst Group has also, since 1985, acquired the Northern Ireland firm Town and

Country Fuels. In all it has a fleet of over 20 oil tankers ranging from the small 17 ton vehicle up to 32 ton articulated vehicles. In 1992 Hurst's began making supplies to some 36 BP petrol stations.

It is also worth noting that to this day the banking facilities enjoyed by T.B.F. Thompson Ltd. and Charles Hurst Ltd. are "unsecured". "T.B.F." is in the position - possibly unique - of not having had to offer any personal guarantees or charges, either fixed or floating, to the Northern Bank for his various personal and business ventures. Although "T.B.F." has always maintained a close relationship with and loyalty to the Northern Bank, in recent years further developments have seen him become involved with the Bank of Ireland, First Trust and the Ulster Bank. In connection with the Ulster Bank he and Mr. Ronnie Kells, who is not only an excellent Chief Executive, but also an excellent after dinner speaker and story teller, have a rather unusual business arrangement, in that if "T.B.F." uses one of the stories which he has heard Mr. Kells tell, then "T.B.F." would be required to introduce some business to the Ulster Bank. This arrangement would appear to be mutually advantageous! - but that is another story!

The lines of "Wee Johnny Funny" spoken by Tom with the Garvagh Christmas Rhymers so many years before had proved more accurate than "T.B.F." could ever have dreamt:

"Here come I - Wee Johnny Funny,
I'm the man that takes the money.
All silver - no brass,
Bad ha'pence won't pass."

So it was that "T.B.F.'s" powers of concentration, backed by the support of his colleagues, in going after Hurst's was a huge success. It was the milk in the coconut, for sure. But life holds its surprises and "T.B.F." was, as 1990 dawned, about to get some of the biggest surprises of his life.

Charles Hurst Limited

Seated (from left): Main Board Directors: Messrs Gordon Scott, Fred Maguire, Frank Shaw, Ken Surgenor.
Back row (from left): Subsidiary Directors: Messrs Jim McAlees, Tom Wilson, Hugh Gordon, Ronnie Crooks,
Richard Stinson, Terry Halliday, Tom Magowan and Colin McNab

McLaughlin & Harvey Construction Ltd.
Seated (from left) Main Board Directors: Messrs Stephen Hamill, Gilbert Watson.
Back row (from left): Divisional Directors: Messrs Trevor Charlesworth, Raymond Doggart, Ronnie Stewart
Inset: Robert Hampton

◆ CHAPTER SIXTEEN ◆

"A maroon Jaguar"

"**T**HE VAN" CAME TRUNDLING DOWN THE ROAD. No, it wasn't a modern vehicle bought from a Charles Hurst Centre. It had one-horse power and the driver sat in his seat on the top of the covered wagon, as he always did, whether it rained or snowed, urging his horse forward.

His name was Andrew Lamont, a local farmer, and he had a contract with the Northern Ireland Department of Education to convey children within a five mile radius to their local school. It was early in the 1940s and coming walking down to what was known as "The New Line" to the pick-up point, came a little girl called Betty, daughter of James and Anna Kelly who lived locally at the Camus. Betty stepped up on to the little step at the back of the van and sat down amongst her school friends.

The horse started off and the children started chatting among themselves. It was a Friday and Friday was test day at school and Master Millar, known to all and sundry as Curly Tam, tested his class on all that he and his excellent assistant, Miss

Winifred Murdock, affectionately known as "Winnie" had been teaching that particular week.

The children noticed, though, that Harry McDermott was somewhat apprehensive. He was swaying back and forward on the seat and rubbing his hands. The children heard him keep mumbling words to himself and before long the words became very distinct. Over and over Harry said, "I wish I was here coming back again!.... I wish I was here coming back again!..... I wish I was here coming back again!"

"I wish I was here coming back again" proved to be a very relevant phrase for the little girl seated beside Harry, for her life was later to be filled with hectic schedules, great responsibilities, and some fairly formidable public occasions in which she was to play a very important part. The most important of all, of course, was to be the part she was to play in the life of T. B. F. Thompson. Betty's childhood was a very happy one on her parent's small farm at the Camus by the gently flowing River Bann. Her childhood memories are filled with images of forty shades of green across the County Londonderry rural landscape and memories of helping her aunt with meal baskets carried to men working in fields of golden grain at harvest time.

Often she would jump the stones on the flax dam and well remembers the fierce consequences when her foot slipped!

Betty, with her brother David, regularly walked to the Ballylaggan Reformed Presbyterian Church to the services and Sabbath School, some four miles distant. She did this regularly, spring, summer, autumn and winter and her life was deeply influenced by the minister, Rev. A. R. Wright. Mrs. Wright also showed a very keen interest in the children and young people of the church and Betty came to personal faith in Christ as Saviour and Lord early in life. In those far-off days the highlights of a year would have been the Sabbath School excursion at the beginning of July and the Congregational Social at the beginning of February. The Sabbath School excursion meant walking to Coleraine and then catching a steam train from Coleraine Station to Portrush, by the sea. There were races and games on the Strand and Barry's Amusements were kept busy!

Some of Betty's earliest memories are of her brother Robert coming home at week-ends from Stranmillis Teachers' Training College and of the rambles she, David and Robert would take together. Many were the miles, too, that Betty and David cycled across the country to visit friends and the homes of aunts and uncles. They loved to cross the Agivey Bridge over the River Bann and to stop half way across with the front wheel in Co. Antrim and the back wheel in Co. Londonderry.

The Covenanter Young People's Union was regularly attended and there an opportunity was given to meet with other young people and strong emphasis placed on development in the Christian life.

After attending Castleroe Public Elementary School, Betty left the care of Master Millar and Miss Murdock and was transferred to the Model Primary School in Coleraine where Dr. J. K. Forbes was the Principal and Miss Georgina Woodrow was the Vice Principal. As well as the usual school subjects Betty developed a keen interest in verse speaking and choral singing and was deeply involved with the school choir. In 1951 Miss Woodrow and Miss Lee took the school choir on a very memorable trip to London to tour the Festival of Britain site at Battersea. Arrangements were also made for the choir to attend performances of "H.M.S. Pinafore" by the D'Oyly Carte Opera Company, and "1066 and All That", as well as a trip to the ballet.

Betty's school studies continued at Coleraine Technical College and towards the end of her time there her father sadly died just a week before she was due to sit her "Senior" examination. Her father's death had a deep effect on her because he had not only been a good father but he had been a wise counsellor and friend.

His passing was felt all the more keenly because the family had just moved from the country to live in Coleraine, some two months prior to his death. Her brother David was now teaching in the Irish Society School in Coleraine and it meant a lot to have David at home.

Betty's interest in choral singing continued through membership of the renowned Coleraine Linnets Ladies' Choir, for many years under the leadership of Mr. James Moore and Miss Mavis Christie. The Linnets Choir sang at many concerts throughout the country, including a tour of Scotland in 1956 and took part in various competitions at local Music Festivals and also participated on radio. In 1954 Betty joined the choir of the Northern Presbytery of the Reformed Presbyterian Church and remained a member over many years. This choir, conducted by her cousin, Mrs. Kathleen Wright, celebrated its 40th anniversary in 1994.

In 1956, through having completed a course at Coleraine Technical College, Betty qualified as a Pitman's Shorthand teacher. Later that year she went to Scotland to gain some experience in teaching and taught at Kirkcaldy High School and Viewforth Secondary School. She also taught for a short time at Skerries College at Edinburgh and at the Astley Ainsley Hospital School in Morningside, Edinburgh. At this time Betty stayed with her Aunt Mary and cousin Nancy Anderson in Kirkcaldy.

Unfortunately Betty's mother's health began to suffer and she came back home to take up a position as Private Secretary to the Manager in the Ballantyne Knitwear Company in Coleraine. Ballantyne's are the manufacturers of fine cashmere and lambswool knitwear in the border counties of Scotland. Betty remained at Ballantyne's until she left to go to Garvagh in 1970, commencing on 2nd November as private and confidential secretary to the Chairman of T. B. F. Thompson (Garvagh) Ltd. In July 1971, she and her mother came to live in Garvagh in one of the company houses in Thompson Crescent and as T. B. F. Thompson continued to expand his business interests her job as secretary became more varied and very challenging. She developed a great respect for "T.B.F." and admired his high ideals in his business practice and the importance that he placed upon people. To say that he kept a very full diary is an understatement and she recalls that when in 1975 Dr. John Haggai visited Ulster for a special mission, Dr. Haggai wanted "T.B.F." and his wife to visit him at his headquarters in Atlanta, Georgia. When "T.B.F." indicated that he could not fit it into that year's programme and showed him his diary, John Haggai turned to Betty and said, "I guess with T. B. F. Thompson you either take pep pills and keep going on with him, or you take sleeping pills and forget all about him!"

From the beginning Betty had a very good relationship with Mrs. Kathleen Thompson who often gave her sound advice over the years on many matters which proved most helpful. In 1979 when "T.B.F." and his wife Kathleen set up their Trusts, Betty was honoured to be chosen as one of the Chief Trustees and the development of the activities within these Trusts has continued to be one of the most interesting parts of her life.

The respect and affection that Betty had for "T.B.F." began to grow into something deeper after he had asked her out for dinner on her birthday in September 1989. Soon they were into something which, as they say, was "bigger than both of them"! On the 16th May, 1990 they were married at a special wedding ceremony at the Conway House Hotel in Dunmurry. The best man was a former Moderator of the Presbyterian Church in

Ireland, Dr. John Girvan and his wife, Mary, was matron-of-honour. The Rev. David McKay, assisted by Rev. Stanley Lindsay, officiated at the ceremony. It was a very quiet wedding and the whole business group that "T.B.F." directed had no notion what was up.

Soon after the wedding a maroon Jaguar slipped on to the Irish ferry which headed for Stranraer; it then slipped off the ferry and was driven on to the lovely Turnberry Hotel with its golf courses and its magnificent view of the Clyde and Ailsa Craig. A lone piper piped guests into dinner and two of them were Mr. and Mrs. T. B. F. Thompson.

The honeymoon was, they thought, a virtual secret but the police, it turned out, had an eye on it. On the Monday of the week following their marriage, a Secretary in the T.B.F. Thompson organisation had a phonecall from the Strathclyde Police checking out details on a certain Mr. and Mrs. T. B. F. Thompson. Were they the owners of a maroon Jaguar? Was their address "Heathlands", 21 Station Road, Garvagh? Were they both in Scotland at this time? The Secretary could confirm that as far as she knew Mr. T. B. F. Thompson was in Scotland and, yes, 21 Station Road was his address. The maroon Jaguar certainly belonged to her boss.

What had happened was that a NATO conference was about to be held at Turnberry Hotel and the Foreign Secretaries of many European states were arriving from all over the Continent; the Prime Minister, Margaret Thatcher, was opening the conference and the police were checking out all Irish people moving in and out of the Turnberry area. They had to be sure that Mr. & Mrs. T. B. F. Thompson were not about to blow the place apart! As it was, "T.B.F." and Betty's cover was blown and oblivious to all of this they went on to stay at the Gleneagles Hotel in Perthshire for a few days. Soon they slipped back on to the ferry and sailed home to be greeted by the delight of their friends as news of their marriage broke.

No sooner were they home than it was time for the Balmoral Show, Northern Ireland's premier agricultural show of the year. They were pleased to sit down with leading members of the Royal Ulster Agricultural Society to dinner. The news of their marriage was out and "T.B.F." and Betty could at last drive the maroon Jaguar in peace!

"T.B.F." and Betty on the occasion of his graduation as a Doctor of Science at Queen's University Belfast, July 4th 1990.

*"T.B.F." and Betty at "Heathlands" with Mr. Andrew Magowan
(Managing Director of TBF Thompson (Garvagh) Ltd,)
and his wife, Betty.*

*The "at home" at "Heathlands", August 23rd, 1990
during "T.B.F.'s" year as High Sheriff for the County of
Londonderry. From left: Mrs. Mulholland, Mr. Richard Mulholland
(High Sheriff for the County of Londonderry for 1989),
Lt. Col. Michael McCorkell O.B.E., T.D. (Lord Lt. for the County of
Londonderry, now Sir Michael McCorkell K.C.V.O),
Mrs. Eaton, Mr. James Eaton (High Sheriff, for the City of
Londonderry), "T.B.F." and Mrs. McCorkell (now Lady McCorkell).*

"T.B.F." becomes an Officer of the Order of the British Empire, December 10th 1990. Also in the picture at Buckingham Palace Betty (left) with friend, Miss Irene Wright.

"T.B.F." and Betty at Heathlands.
(Photo: Bob Little, Toronto)

162

The Board of Govenors, Coleraine Academical Institution in the year of "T.B.F.'s" retirement as a governor in 1993.

♦ CHAPTER SEVENTEEN ♦

"It was a very good year"

A LOT OF OLDER PEOPLE VIEW AGING WITH A growing discontentment rather than acceptance. The jokes about it are pretty predictable. You know you are getting older when:

You get out of the shower and you are glad the mirror is all fogged up.

The airline attendant offers you "coffee, tea or Milk of Magnesia".

Your actions creak louder than words.

You view the seven ages of man as spills, drills, thrills, bills, ills, pills, wills.

You sink your teeth into a juicy steak and they stay there.

You get to greener pastures and you cannot climb the fence.

You start using a shaving lotion for the over 65's called "Old Spouse".

You sit down on a rocking chair and you can't get it started.

The truth is, though, for "T.B.F." it was not wintertime in his life, it was harvest. The principles he had lived by were now, in fact, bearing a remarkable harvest.

In 1987 "T.B.F." had been approached by the Northern Ireland Office to see if he would be willing to accept the position of High Sheriff for County Londonderry. High Sheriffs are appointed by the Lord Lieutenants of Counties within the United Kingdom on behalf of Her Majesty The Queen, to officially help them in their work. They are, while in office, the Head Magistrate in a County. It is a position of very high honour for the citizen of any County.

While High Sheriffs do not play any part in a judicial court case, they can make helpful comment, privately, to the Judge drawn from their knowledge of the County to help him in his deliberation. They are, if you like, the people's representative and show by their presence that justice is being done in the County. The position of High Sheriff goes back to the 13th century.

"T.B.F." felt deeply honoured to be invited to be High Sheriff of his native County and had been given some time to think about the appointment. He had a very real problem with it. The problem lay over his long-standing promise never to buy anyone alcoholic drink. Should he waive his principle on this occasion?

He felt, before God that he dared not and, taking courage in hand wrote the following letter to the Northern Ireland Office on 18th April, 1988. He stated:

"Over the intervening months since receiving your letter there has been one point which has concerned me, and which might cause some embarrassment during my proposed term of office as High Sheriff for the County of Londonderry. I feel, therefore, that it would be better to air the matter now - hence this letter to you.

"Whilst hospitality is a natural function of such an office - and that does not trouble me in the slightest - I have to state that for many years since personally committing my life to Jesus Christ it has been a strongly held principle of mine - both in my business and private life - that I do not consume any alcoholic beverage, nor provide such beverage for others. If it were to be considered that this might cause embarrassment to those with whom I, as High Sheriff, would come into contact, then I would have to abide by my Christian principle and, to my regret, would have to decline acceptance of this honour.

"Subject to this, I would - if appointed - do my utmost to fulfil the obligation of High Sheriff for the County of Londonderry in the high tradition expected of that office.

"I would appreciate your comments in the light of the foregoing."

When the response to his letter eventually came from the representative of the Northern Ireland Office "T.B.F." was very touched to read the following paragraph:

"You were concerned about possible embarrassment during your proposed term of office as High Sheriff which might arise from your strongly held principle of not consuming alcoholic beverages or providing such for others. I can assure you that your desire to abide by this principle would not cause any embarrassment to those with whom you would, as High Sheriff, come into contact; indeed I am quite sure everyone would have the utmost respect for your stance. It is certainly not a requirement of the Office that alcoholic drinks must be provided. I hope you find this reassuring."

He certainly did and was duly appointed High Sheriff for the County of Londonderry for the year 1990.

It is customary after a High Court hearing for the High Sheriff of the County to entertain the visiting High Court Judge and his associates together with local dignitaries. "T.B.F." following his earlier decision, did not serve alcoholic beverage at the luncheon that followed the morning's hearing. As it happened the High Court hearing on this occasion turned out to be a case of manslaughter which was, sadly, related to alcoholic drink. "T.B.F." found the coincidence highly significant.

"T.B.F." may have been surprised to have been appointed as High Sheriff for County Londonderry but to have conferred on him, in the Summer of 1990, the honorary degree of Doctor of Science in Economics by the Queen's University of Belfast truly "knocked him for six"! He who had mitched school and fled its strictures in youth, became Dr. T.B.F. Thompson. It was an event he had never even dreamt would come his way.

He and Betty were invited with all the other Honours Graduands for dinner at the Vice Chancellor's Lodge on Tuesday evening, July 2nd. They also attended a dinner at the Great Hall at Queen's University on Wednesday evening, July 3rd and on Thursday afternoon, July 4th, in the Sir William Whitla Hall the "Bee Charmer" became a Doctor of Science.

Let the citation of Professor Leslie Clarkson on the presentation of "T.B.F.'s" degree speak for itself. He said:

"The journey of Thomas Bacon French Thompson to the spot where he now stands commenced some years ago in Garvagh, County Londonderry, a town described in 1837 as having the 'appearance of great respectability'. After schooling in Garvagh and Coleraine, followed by some years working for his father, a local general merchant, Thomas Thompson entered the transport and haulage business in 1949. An account of his business activities convinces me that Mr. Thompson personally delivers my central heating oil, services my car and even repairs its body work after it has been chipped by stones taken from his quarries and laid on roads constructed by the heavy plant and machinery that he supplies. For our honour graduand is chairman of T.B.F. Thompson Ltd., of Garvagh and Coleraine, and director of the Charles Hurst Group of Belfast. These enterprises between them embrace motor cars and bicycles, heating oils and financial services, earth-moving plant and machinery, quarrying and building. His business empire extends from Garvagh to Gravesend and directly employs over 2600 people and generates a further 1000 through sub-contracting.

"There is another dimension to the life of Thomas Bacon French Thompson. He is director of the Ulster Clinic and of Advanced Medical Technology Ltd., a company that assists medical research in the Queen's Medical School and the Musgrave Park Hospital. At his own expense he supplied defibrillators to doctors and hospitals and supported the cardiac unit of the Waveney Hospital, Ballymena and the Parkanaur Training Centre at Donaghmore. These activities are the outward and visible signs of an inner religious faith that leads him into a strong commitment to the community. In 1978 he formed the Mr. & Mrs. T.B. F. Thompson Trusts to develop charitable works and established the T.B.F. Thompson Ministries. Their scope includes a holiday home at Portstewart where every year 500 needy people are provided with a week's holiday free of charge; a full-time husband-and-wife team who visit the elderly and sick in the community and in hospital, cheering them with cassette players, tapes and literature; and an auditorium seating 200, opened in Garvagh in 1986, complete with restaurant and resident cook, for use by church groups, youth organisations and other community groups. Garvagh still has 'the appearance of great respectability'.

"These are admirable achievements, but in this present context they prompt two questions. The first is, why do they merit the award of a degree in economics? The second question is larger still. Why should a university devoted to a life of learning, recognise success in business and service through philanthropy by the highest degree it has to offer?

"The great English economist, Alfred Marshall, writing in 1890, defined economics as 'a study of mankind in the ordinary business of life.' It is, he continued, 'on the one side a study of wealth; and on the other, and more important side, a part of the study of man. For man's character has been moulded by his every-day work, and the material resources that he thereby procures, more than by any other influence unless it be that of his religious ideals; and the two great forming agencies of the world's history have been the religious and the economic.' Those of you about to graduate in economics, believing it to be a matter of mathematics and cost curves, might be surprised at this definition, but then, who reads Marshall these days? Thomas Thompson, as far as I know, has neither studied economics nor read Marshall's Principles, but he will recognise immediately that his business and religious quests exactly exemplify what Marshall had in mind. He has for decades, without knowing it, been pursuing the discipline of economics.

"Turning to the larger question, the answer is not so very hard to find. Universities do not stand apart from the societies that they seek to serve. We strive through our scholarship and our teaching to enhance all that is humane in society. The humane includes success in business, for by providing employment for many and material goods and services for many more, the community is enriched by the generation of wealth. Humane principles embrace also the pursuit of non-material values for we do not live by motor cars alone. We recognise in the life of our honorary graduand those ideals which inspire universities.

"These are exciting times for Mr. Thompson. He married in May. He was honoured by the award of an O.B.E. in June. In July he receives an honorary doctorate from Queen's University. What the future months have in store I do not know, but we await with interest.

"Vice-Chancellor of the University, by the authority of the Senate, I ask you to confer on Thomas Bacon French Thompson, the degree of Doctor of Science in Economics, honoris causa."

To say that 1990 was a busy year for "T.B.F." and Betty is an understatement. After the graduation at Queen's University they attended a Garden Party at Buckingham Palace on July 19th. Invited by the Lord Chamberlain on behalf of Her Majesty The Queen they flew to London and mixed with about 7,000 others inside the spacious grounds of the Palace, sipping tea with the Queen.

On August 23rd "T.B.F." and Betty were very pleased to be host and hostess of the High Sheriff's annual social gathering. It was held at "Heathlands" and people from public life all across the County of Londonderry were invited, including the Heads of Police, the Lord Lieutenant of the County, the High Sheriff of the City of Londonderry and others.

"T.B.F.'s" and Betty's minds now began to turn to the next major event of the year. As Professor Clarkson had said, "T.B.F." had indeed been announced in Her Majesty's Official Birthday Honours List during the month of June. The London Gazette had printed "T.B.F.'s" name, and officially, he could now use the appropriate letters for the award after his name.

The award of The Order of the British Empire was first instituted by King George V during the Great World War when no suitable award existed to reward the great number of people doing outstanding work. Memories of that Great War had been very close to Mrs. Betty Thompson when she accompanied "T.B.F." to the November 11th Armistice Service at Coleraine. As she watched her husband laying the wreath her mind was filled with deep emotion because her uncle, David Adams had been killed in the First World War. Betty's mother had grieved for her brother's death for most of her life and every year when the Broadcast Remembrance Service from the Royal Albert Hall came around, Mrs. Kelly found it very difficult to watch or listen to the Last Post being played after the symbolic petals had fallen on the hushed congregation.

To receive an honour at Buckingham Palace at an Investiture is to receive recognition by the Queen for personal accomplishment. It is a very fitting climax to an outstanding career and, truth is, it is not in the getting of an award but in the deserving that the honour lies.

By any stretch of the imagination, Dr. T. B. F. Thompson thoroughly deserved his award.

Flying from Aldergrove Airport "T.B.F.", Betty and her life-long friend Irene Wright checked in at the Royal Westminster Hotel in London on the evening of December 9th.

In the morning they were up bright and early and soon a chauffeur driven Daimler arrived at the front of the Royal Westminster to take them to Buckingham Palace for the 11 o'clock Investiture. At 10.50 a.m. a detachment of the Yeomen of the Guard, first established by Henry VII in 1485, resplendent in their Tudor uniforms, marched into the ballroom where Betty and Irene and the rest of the families of that morning's 130 recipients were seated. At the stroke of 11 o'clock the Queen arrived and the Investiture began.

It was all very pleasant for those watching as a small orchestra from one of the Guard's Regiments played in the Minstrel's Gallery. "T.B.F.", though, found the resplendent pomp and ceremony impressive, if somewhat daunting. Briefed by a Lieutenant Colonel in the Palace's Picture Gallery "T.B.F." was desperately trying to remember his instructions, clearly.

"Go forward and stop by the Gentleman Usher", the Lieutenant Colonel had said, "When you hear your surname read by the Lord Chamberlain, go forward to the middle of the room until you are level with the Queen. Turn left, bow, and go forward to the edge of the dias where the Queen is standing (don't get on the dias; repeat, don't get on the dias!). The Queen will put the medal on the hook provided, speak to you for a moment or two and when she puts out her hand to shake yours, that is the signal to go. Step back to the middle of the room, turn right out of the ballroom and turn right out of the ballroom door. You will be shown to a small room where your medal will be promptly taken away from you. Don't worry, in a few moments you will get it back in a box!"

"T.B.F.'s" head was beginning to spin a little. What was it? "Go forward to the middle of the room ....". Suddenly the Lieutenant Colonel's voice said with laughter, "If you forget all that, just follow the person in front of you and do what they do.

Of course, that's fine unless the person is a lady and she'll be doing a curtsey!"

"T.B.F." got to the dias, safely, and in a very special and personal moment received his honour from the Queen.

When, at last, the trio had cleared the Palace gates they headed straight to the House of Lords for lunch with their friend Lord Blease. Lunch soon stretched into afternoon tea. It was all a superb follow-up to the morning of a lifetime.

"T.B.F." and Betty rounded off December 1990 by spending Christmas in Austria. As the gentle snow fell across the forests and ski slopes, the villages, the cities and the towns, "T.B.F." and Betty reflected on what had been, by any account, an extraordinary year. They were humbled and grateful that they were privileged to have enjoyed it together. Their wish for everyone born out of long experience could best be summed up in the Christmas wish of the late Bishop Remington. He once wrote:

"I am wishing you this day a Happy Christmas.
I would send you those gifts which are beyond price,
outlast time and bridge all space.
I wish you all laughter and pure joy, a merry heart and
a clear conscience, and love which thinks no evil,
is not easily provoked and seeks not its own;
The fragrance of flowers, the sweet associations of
holly and mistletoe and fir, the memory of deep woods,
of peaceful hills, and of mantling snow, which guards the
sleep of all God's creatures.
I wish the spirit of Christmastide may draw you
into companionship with Him who giveth all.
Come, let us adore Him".

*Mrs. Lena England unveils the plaque in the presence of "T.B.F."
and the Very Rev. Dr. John Girvan, who dedicated the Ministries to
the glory of God and in memory of Mrs. Kathleen L. Thompson.*

The Memorial plaque.

At the opening of TBF Thompson Ministries Auditorium and suite of offices, 1st November, 1986. From left: Mr. Vernon Arbuthnot, Very Rev. Dr. William A. Craig, Miss Betty Kelly, "T.B.F.", Mrs. Lena England (sister of the late Mrs. Thompson), Very Rev. Dr. John Girvan and Mr. Edward McBriar.

The TBF Thompson Ministries Team. From left, back row: Mrs. Joy Arbuthnot, Mr. James McIlroy, Mrs. Joan Watt, Mrs Doreen Dinsmore. Seated, from left: Mrs. Hazel Hargy, Mr. Vernon Arbuthnot.

*Part of the Trinity Room Restaurant at the TBF Thompson Ministries Headquarters
in Garvagh with its beautiful mirror mural.*

*The Rock House Holiday Home staff. From left: Mrs. Moira Penny, Mr. Sam Irons,
Mrs. Joyce Dinsmore and, seated, Mrs. Anna Irons.*

*"T.B.F." is presented with an Illuminated Address on his retirement
as president fo the Garvagh C.W.U. on 10th March 1994.
From left: Mrs. Betty Magowan, Mrs. Rose Hutchinson,
Mrs Helen Rodgers, Mr. Derick Bingham, Rev. Dr. A. R. Rodgers,
"T.B.F.", Mr. Campbell Hutchinson, Mrs. Betty Thompson,
Mr. James McIlroy and Mrs. Joy Arbuthnot.*

*"T.B.F." with Vernon Arbuthnot who took over the Presidency of
Garvagh C.W.U. on 10th March, 1994*

The first Thompson commercial building in Garvagh built in the 1930's for £100. It consisted solely of the little building behind the double doors to the extreme left of this photograph.

The site of TBF Thompson (Garvagh) Ltd as it is today.

*On the occasion of the presentation of gold watches as awards for long service with T.B.F. Thompson (Garvagh) Ltd.,
12th April, 1995. From left: back row, Messrs. John McShane, William Patterson, Jack Graham, Fred Smyth, Jim
Convery, Jim Boyce, Sam Woodward, Peter Lagan, Ken Neely. Front row, seated: Mr. Brian Webb,
Mr. Raymond Campbell, Mrs. Sandra Campbell, "T.B.F.", Mr. R. J. Gillanders, Miss Anona Dillon,
Mrs. Mary Magilligan, Mr. Sandy Gray, Mr. Andrew Magowan (Managing Director)
T.B.F. Thompson (Garvagh) Ltd.*

The Headquarters of the TBF Thompson Ministries (front part of building).

Betty and "T.B.F" in his office with his personal secretary Mrs. Alison Kelly.

◆ CHAPTER EIGHTEEN ◆

"And the future?"

"T.B.F." IS NOW LOOKING FORWARD, IN THE WILL of God, with keen anticipation to a string of new projects. He is as busy as ever. The red lights on the hi-tech switchboard at his headquarters blink incessantly. Secretaries keep his projects on track and those projects are significant.

In November, 1993 "T.B.F." and his colleagues came to the aid of one of Northern Ireland's leading Building and Civil Engineering Contractors, McLaughlin & Harvey Ltd., which was, at that time, in the hands of the receivers. They bought the assets of the company and formed a new one named McLaughlin & Harvey Construction Ltd. Ninety-one jobs were saved. The company is now employing one hundred and five employees with 500+ employees in sub-contracting.

Again the old principles "T.B.F." has lived by are surfacing; an extract from the Minutes of a board meeting at McLaughlin & Harvey Construction Ltd. on 25th January 1994, proves it. A statement from "T.B.F." was read to the meeting by Mr. Cheevers as follows:

"On behalf of my colleagues - Mr. R. J. Gillanders, Mr. K. H. Cheevers and myself as owners of the new Company, McLaughlin & Harvey Construction Ltd., it is appropriate that in the course of the meeting with you in this capacity I should indicate two principles by which I endeavour to conduct my life, both privately and in business:

"First, no alcohol is bought or paid for by any Company in which I am involved. Entertaining is welcomed - but alcohol in any shape or form is not - either bought by the Company or by a manufacturer. We wish this policy to be observed.

"Secondly, with regard to Sunday opening and Sunday trading - I believe these to be wrong.

"These two principles are basic in our business approach - they have stood us in good stead over many years in the past, and will do so in the future."

It is interesting that there is a correlation between the life of "T.B.F." and the famous businessman Thomas Cook who opened up the world to the whole idea of package holidays. Cook could have afforded to have done all sorts of things in his life but he preferred to remain in Leicester, England, using his wealth to support those causes, which, as a deeply committed Christian, were dear to his heart, especially to temperance movements.

The successes of his travel agency brought him fame and great personal satisfaction but this only increased his gratitude to God and to the city which was his home and the people who had encouraged him. He was a contented man. Not because the world had become his, but rather because the world which he loved belonged to God. "T.B.F." has a very similar attitude and continues to show great personal interest in the welfare of his native town of Garvagh as well as still holding all kinds of interests throughout Northern Ireland and abroad.

He is living life to the full and to keep up with him, even at this stage of his life, is an exhausting business. His diary is not so much a day planner as a several year planner and it is fascinating to see his desire to keep moving ahead. He is still at "the board" watching his "men" and planning to keep them moving.

The main project of his life at this stage is, of course, the outworking of the Trusts which he and Kathleen formed to provide finance for gospel outreach with the spiritual emphasis towards the needy and more senior members of our society. So much so that he has placed large investments in local Northern Ireland business projects for the benefit of the Trusts, and has transferred at least 80% of his own business interests into the Trusts to ensure their perpetuity.

The first major project of the Trusts was Rock House Holiday Home built at Portstewart in the grounds of "T.B.F.'s" own seaside home.

Rock House Holiday Home is beautifully situated overlooking Portstewart Strand and the distant Donegal hills and it has been of great benefit spiritually, mentally and physically to many in need of, but unable to afford, a restful holiday by the sea. In a year free holidays are provided for over 500 people. Over the years dedicated staff have ensured every comfort and attention for the guests.

Under the Mrs. Kathleen L. Thompson Trust a Public House in Garvagh was purchased, the license surrendered and a work established for youth of the town and district. Known as the Cornerstone, this is now run under the auspices of the YMCA.

Over the years "T.B.F." and Kathleen had a ministry in the distribution of Gospel tracts and cassettes as a means of communicating the Gospel to those whom they met, both at home and abroad. In order to expand this outreach, the TBF Thompson Ministries was formed.

Vernon Arbuthnot was appointed as the first full time worker, and, later joined by his wife Joy, this local couple were employed to visit senior citizens in their own homes, residential homes, nursing homes and hospitals. Video equipment was purchased so that they could show Christian videos in residential homes and Church halls.

In Garvagh, an Auditorium and suite of offices were opened in November 1986 as a memorial to Kathleen L. Thompson who died in July of that year. Seating 200 people, it is fully equipped with organ, piano, and ceiling mounted video projector. It is available to Christian groups, educational and reconciliation groups for day conferences and seminars and evening meetings. In November 1987 the Trinity Room Restaurant was opened to augment and complement the Ministries' outreach. As a result it has been possible to hold dinners for business and professional executives and their partners, with well known public speakers talking about their Christian faith. Promotional dinners for worthy causes have also been held from time to time.

In 1987 Joan Watt (neé Swann) was appointed secretary and in February 1988 James McIlroy was invited to become the Executive Director and head up the rapidly growing organisation. Today he has a staff of nine to help him in the work.

James had been "T.B.F.'s" soloist at the opening of the new Mission Hall in Garvagh and had known him for many years in various avenues of Christian work, and was very happy to accept the responsibility of directing the work of TBF Thompson

Ministries. He has found working with "T.B.F." to be absolutely fascinating and says that with "T.B.F." there is something new every day and life is never dull. He says that he has never met a businessman who is so frank and quick to talk about his Christian beliefs and reckons "T.B.F." is the most courageous Christian witness he has ever had the privilege of knowing.

In 1992 the TBF Thompson Ministries had their 10th Anniversary at a very successful luncheon held in the Cholmondeley Room of the House of Lords. Hosted by Lord Blease of Cromac, it brought together people from across the community in Northern Ireland involved in reconciliation work, with members of the House of Lords such as the Lord Chancellor, Lord Mackay, and the Duke of Norfolk. This provided a wonderful opportunity for constructive discussions on the problems of Northern Ireland. The Ministries look, with great hope, to working for the Lord in a Northern Ireland of permanent peace.

In February, 1994, "T.B.F." resigned, after 45 years, from the Presidency of the Garvagh Christian Workers' Union. His last letter as President sums up how he felt about the future. It read:

"My Dear Friends,

In these days when there is so much uncertainty and insecurity not only here in Northern Ireland but also in many parts of our world I take great comfort from those verses in Romans chapter 8 verses 38 and 39. What a blessing to be assured, as we step into another year, that not even things to come shall separate us from the love of God.

We do not know **WHAT** is in the future but we do know **WHO** is in the future. Christ is in the future. All things come from Him so all things are moving towards Him. The trials God permits in this life, however hard they may seem are within the scope of the "all things work together for good to them that love God"; therefore we may accept in confidence that His grace is sufficient to see us through the most difficult circumstances that may come.

Moreover, let us not forget the privilege and opportunity of bringing everything to God in prayer. In Acts 12:5 we read that when the early Christians were faced with a problem through Peter's imprisonment they prayed with determination and urgency and Peter was free before the end of the prayer meeting.

I have often said that any success I have enjoyed in my business has been because I have prayed for guidance daily and especially before any big decisions had to be made. God did not fail me. I trust and pray that the material blessings I have received from God have enabled me to help others and have been a means of blessing to them too.

Let us go into 1994 with confidence in His continuing love for us and seeking His direction for our paths. If Christ Jesus lives and reigns in our hearts that guidance will be ours.

In February, after 45 years as President, I am resigning and handing over the reins to someone else. I shall of course continue my support for the work of the Lord through the Garvagh CWU but feel that someone younger should carry the responsibility of President. I commend my successor to your prayers and continued support. I wish to thank all my friends who have supported and encouraged me over the years. I have appreciated our fellowship in the Gospel.

Years pass. Times change. Things decay. People die. Dreams vanish. Health fails. Friends leave. But Thou remainest. He is our unchanging Friend.

Through the yesterday of ages
Jesus Thou art still the same
Through our own life's chequered pages
Still the one dear changeless Name
Well may we in Thee confide
Faithful Saviour proved and tried.

A very happy and blessed 1994 to you all.

Yours very sincerely,

T.B.F. THOMPSON"

At the beginning of this book Solomon was quoted as saying, "See a man diligent in his business? He shall stand before kings." Yet, it was the same Solomon, a highly industrious leader himself who wrote, "There was a certain man without a dependent, having neither a son nor a brother, yet there was no end to all his labour. Indeed his eyes were not satisfied with riches and he never asked 'And for whom am I labouring and depriving myself of pleasure?'" (Ecclesiastes 4:1-8)

Who is Solomon addressing? He is talking to entrepreneurs. In the language of our day he is talking to the upwardly mobile, the movers and the shakers, the business moguls, the managing directors and presidents of corporations. He is talking to people who have money and influence and power. He is talking about those who have reached the top of their profession but who never ask, "What is the ultimate outcome of what I am doing?" He sees people who work day and night to get more and more but who are never, ever, satisfied. He is talking to those who forget that they have a soul and that nothing material can ever touch it. They forget that only God can satisfy the needs of the soul through Jesus Christ and that to know Him is to know what the Bible calls eternal life.

"T.B.F." says they are not the "down and outs" but the "up and outs". It is a bit like the very wealthy man who died and someone asked how much he left behind. "He left it all" said a wise onlooker.

In these days "T.B.F." invites to his headquarters at Garvagh leaders from all over the country and has speakers to remind them that gold will not get them into glory and that business done merely for self and money made merely for selfish purposes will turn to dross. He discovered early in life that true success was seeking first the Kingdom of God and His right-eousness and if business acumen is given to anyone, then it is up to them to use it to God's glory and for the good of others, not for their own exclusive use. It is, "T.B.F." claims, the height of folly to climb a ladder of seeming success and then to find that the ladder is up against the wrong wall.

Perhaps the true story of Yussif, the Terrible Turk, may sum up "T.B.F.'s" attitude. He was a wrestling champion in Europe, a while back, and sailed to the United States to fight their champion who gloried in the name of Strangler Lewis. He got the name for his tactic of putting his huge arm around the neck of an opponent and then pumping up his bicep and cutting his opponent's oxygen off at the Adam's apple. His opponent frequently passed out.

The Strangler, though, was soundly beaten by the Terrible Turk for the simple reason that the European had no neck, he just went from his head to massive shoulders! The Strangler simply couldn't get a grip and the Turk went home with $5,000. He insisted, though, in accepting the prize money only in gold.

The Turk strapped the gold around his body and set sail for Europe on the SS BOURGOGNE. Half-way home, the boat sank and Yussif went over the side with his gold still strapped around his body and sank like an anvil before a lifeboat could find him.

It is a tragedy that many people have faced eternity as foolishly as the Terrible Turk faced that Atlantic crossing. They cling to their successes, of whatever kind, never realising that they do not possess their possessions half as much as their possessions possess them. They forget that the Saviour of the world said that a person's life does not consist of the abundance of the things which they possess.

So it was that "T.B.F." found in Jesus Christ the secret of true happiness and he is totally unashamed of owning Christ and pointing others to Him. He discovered through giving that a person can be an overseas missionary without ever leaving their home town, an evangelist without ever mounting a platform, a Bible Teacher without ever writing a book, a comforter without ever entering a hospital, a blessing without ever being seen.

We have come a long way from the days when little Tom Thompson rocked Lord Garvagh's rocking horse at the Imperial Hotel in Garvagh. In those days few people realised the entrepreneurial gifts which were but seedlings in his life when he charged his little friends a penny to see his cinematograph in his mother's kitchen!

Yet, as the decades have rolled by, T.B.F. Thompson has become one of the major entrepreneurs of his generation, giving, through those decades, employment and security to thousands of people. He is to be greatly credited for his achievements in the business world and particularly for his wise management which steered his companies through the formidable economic recession of the 1980's.

"T.B.F." is very quick to recognise that, as the Scriptures put it, promotion "Comes neither from the east nor from the west nor from the south" but from the Lord. He also recognises that what the Bible teaches is not only relevant to eternal salvation, but, that its teaching is vital in the areas of personal honesty, self-control, truthfulness, thrift, industriousness and underlines the importance of taking personal responsibility for one's actions and for the good of the community. Recently a friend discovered that "T.B.F." had rebound his Bible because it was falling apart through frequent use. "T.B.F.'s" friend immediately quipped, "Tom, the man whose Bible is falling apart - isn't!" That truth still stands.

"T.B.F.", for all of his success, is also very quick to recognise and acknowledge that but for the loyal service given by people in his employ in his various business activities over the years he could never have accomplished what he has accomplished. His employees are, however, too numerous to mention within the pages of this book but are remembered with gratitude and much affection. He has often said that "It always comes down to people" and he has been fortunate in gathering good people around him.

This also included a very efficient Housekeeping staff who have cared for the day to day running of his home, extending hospitality to his many visitors, both business and personal. This continues to this day.

He is also particularly grateful to the Medical personnel who have helped him through various illnesses over the years by their skills and kindness.

There is no question that his business acumen has brought great economic benefit, not only to his local town and district, but also to his native Province. When history begins to assess the past decades of life in Northern Ireland, T.B.F. Thompson's name will undoubtedly surface as a significant contributor to its wellbeing.

The great historian Edward Gibbon defined five basic reasons why the civilisation of the Romans, which he so famously chronicled, eventually withered and died. The flaws he detected were an undermining of the dignity and sanctity of the home, the spending of public money for free bread and circuses for the populace, a mad craze for pleasure, with pastimes becoming every year more exciting and immoral, the building of great armaments, although the real enemy was within - the decay of individual responsibility - and, finally, the decay of religion where faith faded into mere form, losing touch with life and losing power to guide people.

T.B.F. Thompson's overcoming, by God's grace, of all five flaws have been the reason why he is still, after over 50 years in business, one move ahead. It is his prayer that whatever years are left to him they may be spent in continuing to seek first the Kingdom of God for he has found that if one has that principle at the centre of one's life, the circumference will take care of itself.

Notes:

Chapter One:
Historical background to Garvagh taken from the written work of, and conversations with, local Garvagh historian Wilbert Patterson.

Chapter Two:
'The Marley Code' from 'Highlights of Yesteryear' by George Walker (Ambassador Press).

Chapter Three:
Source on Henry Ford and his work is 'Ford' by Robert Lacey (Pan Books Ltd.)

Quotation by E. B. White first appeared in 'Farewell to Model T' by G. P. Putnam's Sons in 1936.

Chapter Four:
Quotation by Professor Ivor Kenny is from Meriderth, Nelson and Neck: 'The Practice of Entrepreneurs' I.L.O. 1982 and quoted in 'Out on Their Own' by Ivor Kenny (Gill and Macmillan).

Chapter Eleven:
Source on the life of W.P. Nicholson is from the work 'W.P. Nicholson: Flame For God in Ulster' by Sydney Murray (Published by the Presbyterian Fellowship).

Chapter Fourteen:
Story of the Witnessing Pastor is from 'Eternity' March 1981 by Jeffrey L. Cotter, pp. 22-23.